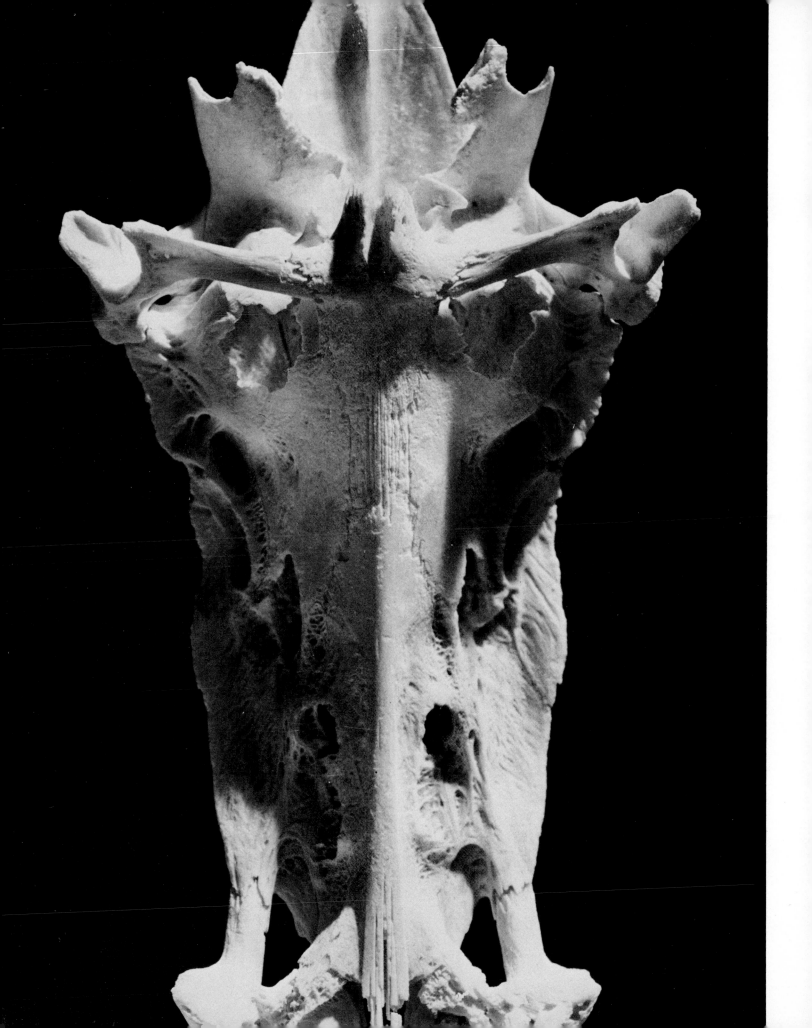

Andreas Feininger

NATURE AND ART

A Photographic Exploration

Dover Publications, Inc.
New York

I dedicate this book to

Loren Eiseley

who, by his thoughts and writings,
has given me more than any other
person, dead or alive.

Frontispiece: Skull of crucifix catfish.

The photographs on the following pages were produced on assignment for LIFE Magazine, are copyrighted by Time, Inc., and are here used with the permission of LIFE Magazine: 54–59, 82, 83, © 1952, Time, Inc; 96, © 1953, Time, Inc.

Published in Canada by General Publishing Company, Ltd., 30 Lesmill Road, Don Mills, Toronto, Ontario.

This Dover edition, first published in 1983, is a revised republication of the work originally published by The Viking Press, New York, in 1975 under the title *Roots of Art: The Sketchbook of a Photographer*.

Manufactured in the United States of America
Dover Publications, Inc., 31 East 2nd Street, Mineola, N.Y. 11501

Library of Congress Cataloging in Publication Data

Feininger, Andreas, 1906–
    Nature and art.

    Rev. ed. of: Roots of art. 1975.
    1. Natural history—Pictorial works. 2. Nature (Aesthetics) I. Title.
QH46.F43   1983   779′.3′0924   83-5250
ISBN 0-486-24539-X

Contents

Foreword

ART = human ability to make things . . . making or doing of things that have form and beauty . . . any craft or its principles . . .

—*Webster's New World Dictionary*
College Edition, 1966

It is in its widest sense that I use the word "art" in the title of this book and the following discussions. For it seems to me that, in the last analysis, everything made by human hands or conceived by the human mind has its roots in nature. To give only two examples: the prototype of the ball-and-socket joint is the hip; the principle underlying a sophisticated system for detecting and locating objects by means of the sound waves they reflect—sonar—was "discovered" aeons ago by bats who use it to target their prey.

But not only can we do *no better* than learn from nature by studying its manifestations, actually this is *the only way* in which we can progress. This is easily proved. The fertile minds of science-fiction writers have created any number of strange worlds populated by the most fantastic creatures. But every single one of their monsters is nothing but a composite of parts borrowed from objects of nature found right here on earth—human, animal or vegetable. This is equally true of gods, angels, devils, mermaids, dragons, unicorns and purple polyps. Not one of these creations of the imagination has features which its originator had not known or seen or heard of before; not one of the colors in which some unearthly landscapes glow is unknown on Earth—because the human mind is inherently incapable of imagining anything of which it has no previous knowledge. The only way to expand our minds is by gaining additional knowledge through further study of nature. It was with this in mind that I originally set out to compile this book.

As the work progressed, however, unexpected things began to happen: I made discoveries in the world of reality as well as in the realm of ideas. It struck me, for example, that symmetry—one of the strongest manifestations of formal artistic organization—was not "discovered" by the builders of ancient monuments but had been used by nature for millions of years in the design of butterflies and thousands of other animals as well as plants. I found pieces of wood shaped by natural forces such as growth, erosion or decay that resembled human faces or figures. I picked up broken shells on the beach that brought to mind classic friezes and sculptures by Henry Moore. I saw landscapes resembling Chinese paintings in the structure of certain stones, and crucifixes in catfish bones. I found pebbles ground and polished by the sea that in geometrical perfection rivaled works by Brancusi and Arp. In short, I discovered similarities between unrelated things which, though entirely fortuitous, linked these objects to one another in my mind and thereby started trains of thought which ultimately culminated in my conviction that nature is the basis of every form of art.

This, of course, is nothing new. But to me, it makes a difference whether knowledge is acquired secondhand—through assimilation of the predigested ideas of other people by means of teaching, reading, discussion, etc.—or gained through firsthand experience. The latter way of learning is ever so much more rewarding and satisfactory because it is the only convincing one. Hearsay can be misleading, but seeing is proof.

There are many ways of "seeing" objects of nature: from the viewpoint of the pragmatist whose only interest is in monetary values—can he sell it, and for how much? Or from the point of view of the economist, whose main concern is whether the objects of his investigations are beneficial or harmful to man. The scientist looks at the objects of nature in a totally different way from that of the artist, the collector in a way different from that of the camera fan whose hobby is nature photography. And so on.

A former architect and structural engineer, I look at objects of nature in two ways: with the eye of a mechanically interested person fascinated by the interrelationship between function and form, and with the eye of an artist in pursuit of what, for lack of a more precise definition, is commonly called beauty.

These interests of mine go back to the days when, as a boy in my early teens, I roamed the hills of Thuringia in Germany in search of fossils and butterflies. They were reinforced when, studying to become an architect, I investigated the connection between function and form from a more pragmatic point of view. And they became a vocation when I finally retired after 20 years of work as a staff photographer for *Life*.

Like all *Life* photographers, I had traveled extensively in the course of my work. As a result, I had encountered many opportunities to pursue my hobby as a

Opposite: Skull of a catfish seen from below. A face with dark and penetrating eyes, a figure with outspread arms, a fetish, an idol, an image of a god . . .

sideline. I had photographed objects of nature that had caught my interest whenever I had a chance, gradually building a collection of photographs which I considered unusual in two respects: in regard to subject matter—rocks, plants and animals selected and photographed specifically to document the influence of function on form and ultimately to prove my assertion that functional forms are ipso facto beautiful; and in regard to the manner in which these objects were "seen," because my engineering background (which enabled me to recognize significant structural features), in conjunction with my art studies and considerable photographic experience, permitted me to present my subjects in what I believe is a particularly informative, stimulating and aesthetically satisfying form.

This is not the first time that I have published a collection of nature photographs in book form. But while my previous books* were documentary in character, presenting their subjects along more or less traditional lines, in this volume I show essentially the same kind of objects seen from a more creative point of view—the viewpoint of the artist, the poet, the dreamer who sees a face in a piece of wood and a crucifix in a fish skull. This approach should make this book attractive, particularly to readers in search of beauty and the hidden connections in life.

Let me try and draw one such connection the way I see it in the form of a parallel between nature and art. A characteristic, not to say indispensable, quality of any work of art is order and structural organization. Underlying this order, and the reason for its being, is an idea, a mental concept, an intangible which the artist had to give concrete form before he could impart his vision to other people. The physical appearance which this form takes depends, of course, on what its creator intended his work to "say"—its meaning, that is: its purpose. Hence, we can say that the tangible form of any work of art is dictated by purpose.

Now, the same reasoning seems to me applicable to nature, where it becomes especially obvious in her living manifestations. Here, the "idea"—the purpose— is survival. Depending upon the specific needs required to assure survival under specific conditions, nature gives its creations and their components specific forms: form becomes the tangible expression of purpose. That this is actually so is proven by the fact that scientists, merely by studying the form of, say, a single bone or tooth of an extinct animal, can draw valid conclusions in regard to its

* *The Anatomy of Nature,* Crown Publishers, 1956, reprinted by Dover Publications, Inc., in 1979; *Forms of Nature and Life,* The Viking Press, 1966.

physical appearance and habit of life. I see here a thought-provoking parallel between nature and artist—both accomplish their goals in analogous ways.

Having satisfied myself of the validity of this analogy, I then gave my imagination free rein and found another connection between nature and art. Primitive man, living in a state of ignorance and fear, populated his world with a host of super-natural beings representing the forces of nature. Nobody knew how they looked or who they were. But then, one fateful day, a shaman picked up a piece of wood or a bone and saw that it resembled the human form, or a human head, a face . . . here was an image of a god! An idol, an object deserving of worship, tangible confirmation of an idea: the gods were real! From there on it can have been only a small step to the artificial creation of similar fetishes that could be venerated, thereby securing the shaman's power over his flock. Such may have been the event leading to the birth of sculpture and eventually to Michelangelo . . .

In another instance, a mind slightly ahead of its time may suddenly have realized that color makes flowers and fall leaves beautiful, or that butterflies have beautiful designs on their wings. This flash of insight—the first conscious awareness of the concept of beauty—may have been followed by reasoning: Why shouldn't I beautify myself with color? And out of this chance observation of nature the decorative arts might have been born: first, body paint with ochre and chalk, then body ornamentation with simple designs, then paintings on cave walls . . . the *Mona Lisa,* Picasso's *Guernica* . . .

I consider this volume the equivalent of the sketchbook of an artist—a random collection of observations, impressions, conclusions and thoughts. Readers who look for organization will probably be disappointed; there is very little. For this is not a book that has a beginning, a middle and an end. Nor was it conceived to guide the viewer from the general to the specific. Rather, it is an invitation to browsing where looking should be followed by contemplation. Each picture was chosen with this goal in mind: to stimulate the viewer, show him familiar objects in a new light, make him aware of strange and sometimes inexplicable connec-tions. I want to show the reader that there is more to nature than what immedi-ately meets the eye, that universal principles seem to exist which equally apply to man and beast; that the atoms and molecules that form his body are identical with those that constitute the rocks, the plants, the animals and the stars. And I want him to feel related to all the objects of nature without which none of us could exist—we, apparently superior yet totally dependent human beings, ephemeral fragments of nature, yet parts of the universe.

NATURE AND ART

A Photographic Exploration

Sculpture

Science tells me that the piece of stone shown on the opposite page consists largely of the mineralized remains of crinoids—sedentary, flowerlike marine animals of the phylum Echinodermata, which lived during the Devonian Period some 400 million years ago. The ramifications of this simple statement are thought-provoking.

This chunk of rock—this bas-relief exquisitely sculpted by nature—once was alive with delicate animals which breathed, assimilated food, propagated and, probably, felt hunger, pain and a state of contentment when life was good, aeons ago. These remains are *not* the grim reminder of an avenging flood that all but wiped out sinful humanity a few thousand years ago, as the Bible would have us believe. This is truth. And to me, truth is the one immutable rock in an ocean of uncertainty and change. Like any other human being, I have a need for something permanent. Some people find this reassurance in God. Others, like myself, are still searching. But to find this ultimate truth we must be spiritually free—free from taboos and superstitions, free from dogmas laid down in fear and ignorance and never revised in the light of added knowledge, free to continue the search wherever it may lead. And I am sure—as sure as anybody can ever be of anything—that in the end there will be light, an all-pervading insight illuminating the immense structure of the universe, revealing the rightful place and purpose of man.

But besides this reassuring thought I read another message in this humble piece of stone: it speaks of change—from life to death, from death to burial under mountainous layers of sediment, and from the tomb to resurrection through geologic uplift and erosion. After millions of years, the crinoids once more are brought to light, for the very last time. For if I had not collected this specimen, erosion would have obliterated it grain by grain—*not* to be lost for good, but to be recycled as part of the never-ending drama of life. Eventually, its atoms of carbon and calcium would have found their way into the tissues of living organisms again. They would have been absorbed from the soil by plants which in time would have been decomposed by fungi and bacteria or eaten by animals which in turn would have been consumed by other animals or people, furnishing the building blocks for new forms of life. And the reassuring thought occurs to me that nothing is ever wasted in nature—that somewhere in my body there are atoms that once might have been part of a Sigillaria tree in a Carboniferous forest, a dinosaur, or prehistoric man; and that, when I am gone, the elements of my body may again become part of a plant, an animal, or serve to sustain another human life—a form of resurrection, eternally.

And still another thought occurs to me as I contemplate this fascinating fossil: it is a symbol of change. Change—the only lasting aspect of the cosmos, of being, of life. Change as manifested in two fundamental processes of nature: accretion and erosion. Accretion is equivalent to adding: sediment-laden floods building up the land layer by layer, a tree adding annual rings and thereby increasing its girth, a sculptor modeling a head by adding clay to clay. Erosion is equivalent to taking away: a stream carving a canyon out of a mountainside, a fossil brought to light by the forces of wind and weather, a sculptor chipping away on a marble block to free the form that already exists in his mind. Change—successions of accretion and erosion, of adding and taking away—becomes a tool of creation. Nature as a creator, a sculptor on a cosmic scale, what a beautiful thought! Is it too much to assume that primitive man, inspired by objects of nature fortuitously carved to images in which he saw himself, took his first faltering steps on the road that ultimately led to Michelangelo?

Opposite: Fossilized crinoids. Age—approximately 400 million years.

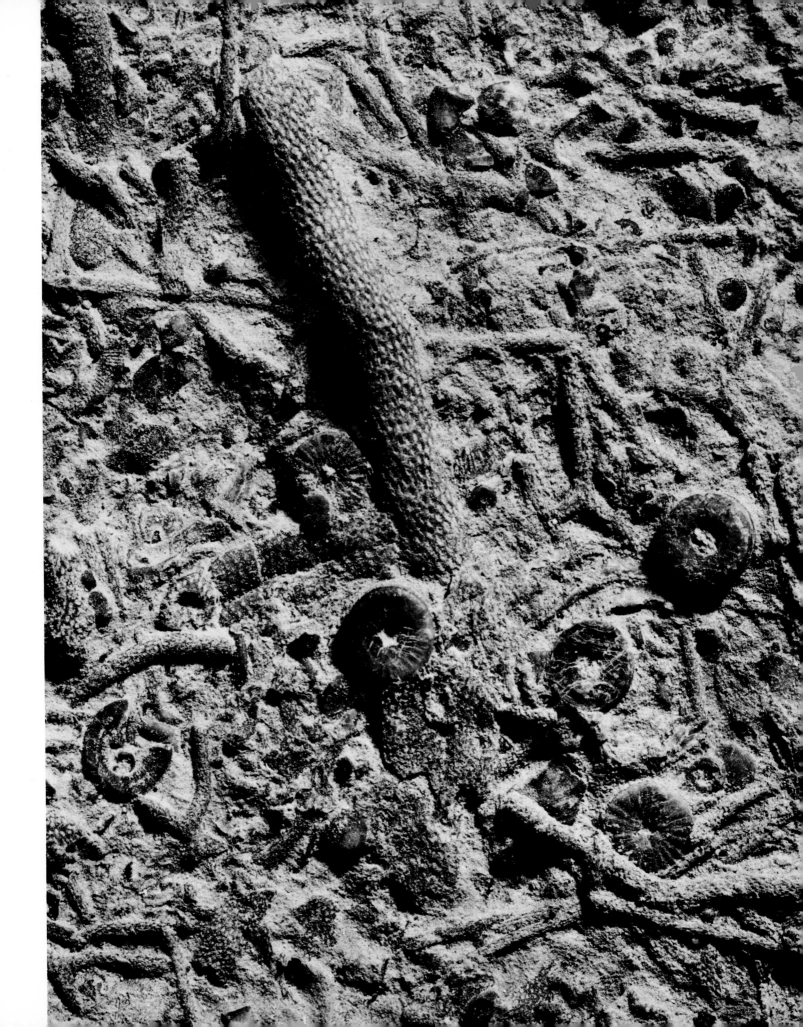

Above: A cow vertebra. *Opposite:* Part of the skeleton of a large bird. Two powerful sculptural forms of nature which, to a primitive and superstitious mind, might have seemed like personifications of the supernatural, demanding appeasement, offerings, worship, supplication . . .

16

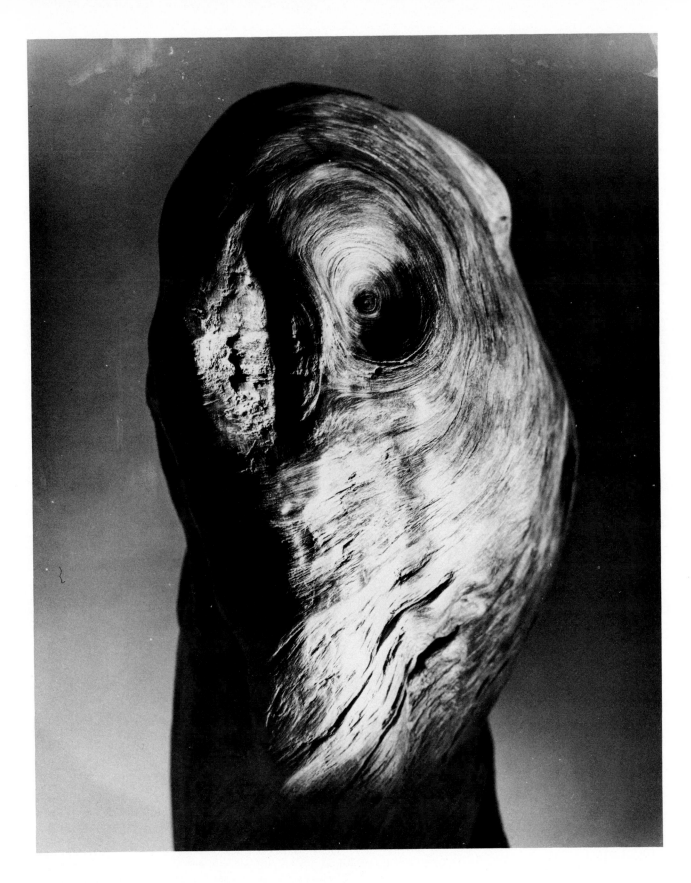

Two forms of nature—pieces of pine roots—untouched by
human hands. A female figure, an embrace, a wood sprite's
face looking at you with owl eyes, embodiment of some of the
forces of nature?

Above: In this pile of basalt I see the statue of a king sitting on his throne, a conqueror overlooking his realm, brooding, menacing . . . In prehistoric times, such a natural form may well have inspired reverence and awe, for who but a god could have created a rock pile in the form of a man? *Opposite:* This malevolent face, complete with eyes, nose and wart, obstinate chin, mouth like a slash—what else could it be but the embodiment of an evil spirit of the forest? Grown naturally, completely untouched by human hands, it formed part of a hollow tree, and I photographed it without changing anything.

Above: Crude stones, piled high and painted black, white and red, form a phallic symbol, the roots of which reach back thousands of years into prehistory. It stands outside the little village of Rödsten in Östergötland, Sweden, originally erected as a tribute to Frö, the Norse god of fertility. Tradition demands that it be repainted every time the farmer paints his barn, otherwise the crops will fail. *Opposite:* Menhirs from the megalithic "alignments" in the Morbihan community near Carnac in Brittany, France. Man's first use of stone on a cyclopean scale was not for housing, defense or any other prosaic purpose, but to express some transcendental concept. What this was is lost in the abyss of time. What we know is that these gigantic monoliths have withstood the ravages of millennia, sometimes standing on tiptoe, the hard way; that they still proclaim their message, although we can no longer understand the language; and that they will probably outlast anything built by modern man. Rough forms of nature, organized by man with thought and purpose, are transformed into works of art.

Above: Jointed granite in the Rockies, split by heat and frost, worn by wind and weather, assumes organic, almost phallic forms. In feeling, these forms are related to those of the "Venus of Willendorf" *(opposite),* the most famous of all the little Ice Age figurines carved by the mammoth-hunters of the Upper Pleistocene some 15,000 years ago. Its generous proportions, round and rich and bountiful, suggest fertility, abundance and earthiness—the image of a mother goddess glorifying the continuity of life.

A reclining figure by Henri Matisse *(above)* and a statue by Gaston Lachaise *(opposite)* are the modern versions of the prehistoric Venus—slicker, more sophisticated, yet spiritually identical concepts of mature femininity created by sculptors whose reaction to woman seems identical with that of Ice Age man.

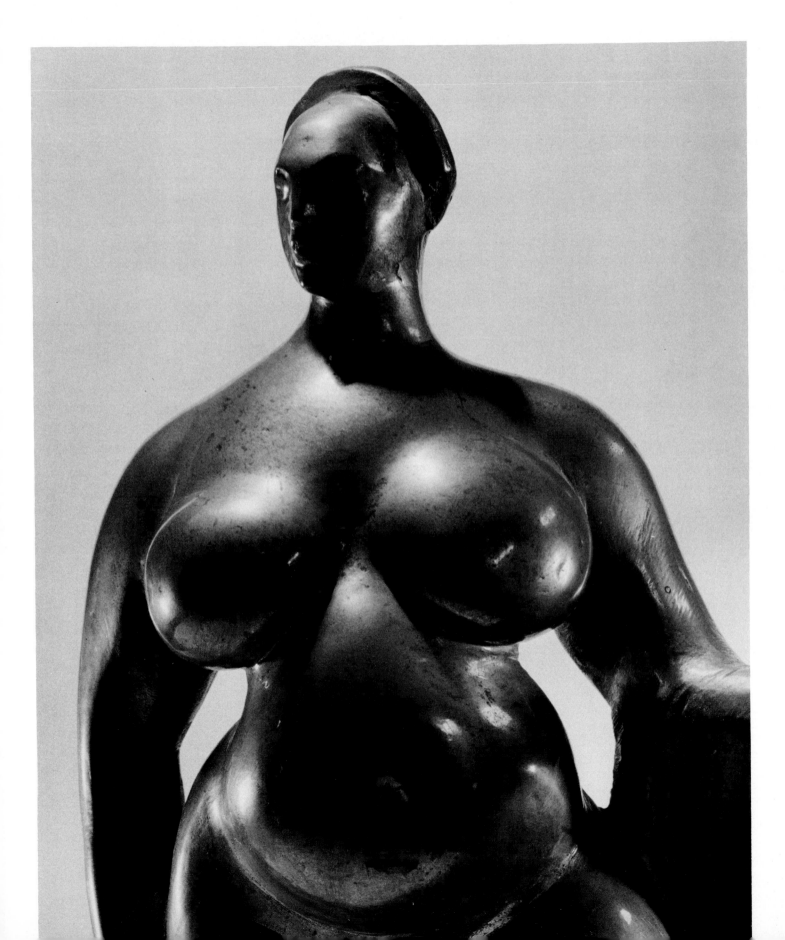

A pre-Columbian clay head from Mexico *(opposite)* and a cap rock protecting a column of softer conglomerate in Utah *(above)*. The resemblance is striking, even though the little head is only an inch and a half high and the natural formation 15 feet high.

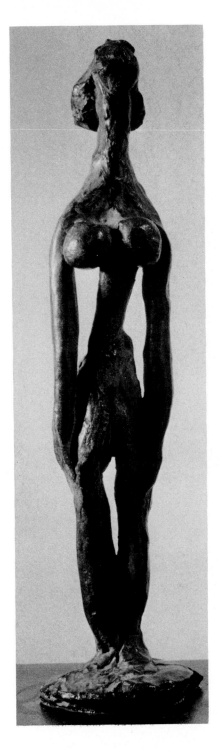  

The fascinating objects on the opposite page were made not by man but by nature. They are concretions—natural aggregates consisting of hardened clay or lime-cemented grains of sand. How they derived their interesting shapes is still not fully understood.

To me, concretions are a source of never-ending stimulation, like three-dimensional Rorschach tests. I see in them people, objects and events, knights in heavy armor, dragons, male and female figurines . . . and I feel a strong emotional relationship between them and the three sculptures by Picasso shown above.

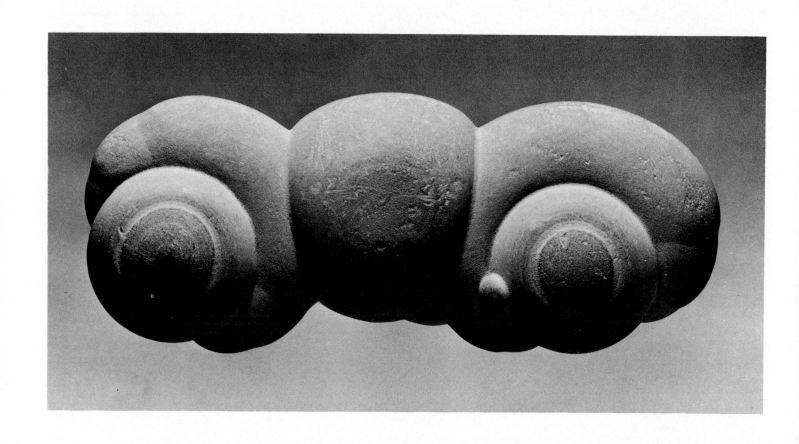

Above: A concretion, a natural form consisting of hardened clay or lime-cemented grains of sand. *Opposite:* Female alabaster figurine from Tepe Hissar, Iran, ca. 1500 B.C. (University Museum, Philadelphia, Pa.; 33-22-92). Evidently abstract creations are neither new nor a prerogative of man.

Above: Rear view of a trapdoor spider. *Opposite:* Head of a gargoyle from the Great Pyramid near Mexico City. The "face" on the armored shield of the spider is only an illusion, the purpose of its design unknown. But it is not difficult to surmise that a pattern similar to this might have inspired the Aztec artisan who carved this monstrous stony head.

Opposite: Egyptian terra-cotta figurine of the predynastic period, ca. 3000 B.C. (Brooklyn Museum, New York; 07-447-502).
Above: Tulip-tree leaves unfolding in spring. The graceful curves of the unfolding leaf stems have their counterpart in the sinuous curves of the little figurine, the head of which suggests a germinating seed about to penetrate the soil. Although the purpose of this little statue is not known, its plantlike forms bring to mind harvesting rites and thoughts of spring and growth.

Above: Woman Reclining by Henry Moore (Museum of Modern Art, New York). *Opposite: Ellipse* by Doris Caesar. To my mind, both works were strongly influenced—perhaps subconsciously—by plant forms. I see in their curves and swelling shapes bulbs, tubers and roots growing and expanding; I sense the dynamic pulsing of life.

Above: Segment of a pine root. *Opposite:* Madonna and Child, Burgundy, fifteenth century. To me, the natural form conveys the same feeling of tenderness and love as the medieval statue.

Above: Close-up of cow vertebrae. *Opposite:* Reclining figure by Henry Moore, Louisiana Museum, Denmark. Skeletal forms in the raw and implied in the disguise of latent yet decisive elements in sculpture.

Above: Sculpture by Henry Moore, Lincoln Center, New York.
Opposite: Cow vertebrae in the desert. The feeling of monu-
mentality depends not so much on size as on form. An object
as small as a bone can have monumental qualities while a
sculpture of heroic size can seem artistically insignificant, as
proven by any number of tasteless war memorials and eques-
trian statues. In the present example, however, the spirit, the
essence, the feeling evoked by the forms of nature and the
work of the artist is essentially the same: strength and power
derived from functional simplicity analogous to the phrase "cut
down to the bone."

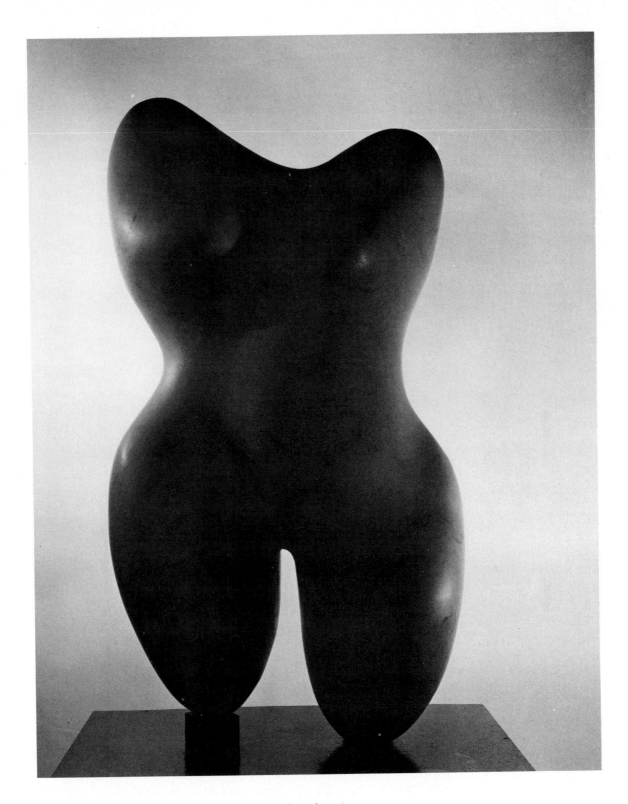

Above: A sculpture by Alberto Viani (Museum of Modern Art, New York). *Opposite:* A stone ground and polished by the sea. The spiritual relationship between these two forms as expressed in the perfection of flowing curves and impeccability of finish is obvious—but if one furnished the model for the other, it was the natural form that was there first. To appreciate fully the sensuous beauty of these two objects they should be explored by touch—hands caressing their silky surfaces while eyes are closed to exclude extraneous distractions.

Above: Marble head from the Cyclades, Greece, second mil-
lennium B.C. (Metropolitan Museum of Art, New York; Guen-
nol Collection). *Opposite: Mother and Child* by Robert Moir
(Whitney Museum of American Art, New York). The roots of
abstract sculpture go very deep indeed.

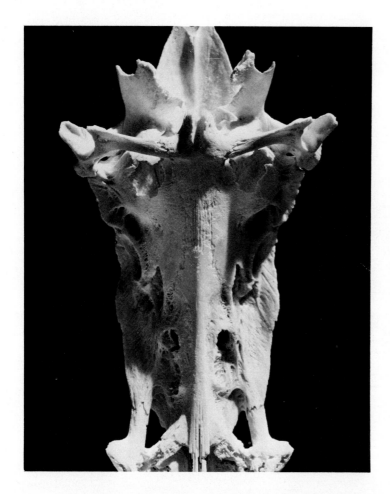 

Above, left: Skull of crucifix catfish. *Above, right:* Iranian figurine from a Bronze Age tomb at Turang-Tepe, ca. 2000 B.C. (University Museum, Philadelphia, Pa.; 32-41-25). *Opposite:* Close-up of a broken shell. Again, a common element unites these sculptural forms: the outstretched arms, the gesture—real or implied—of greeting and welcome. And it would be hard to decide which expresses this feeling more strongly, the forms of nature or the work of man.

Structure

Nothing in nature is structureless. If something seems amorphous or homogeneous, it is only because its structure is too fine to be visible to the naked eye. Even substances as "unstructured" as glass or water are internally organized, consisting of molecules which consist of atoms which in turn consist of a wealth of subatomic particles. Whether or not there is a lower end to structure is not known, although the tenets of quantum physics predict it.

To me, a former architect and engineer, structure in all its forms has a powerful attraction. I see on one side structure, organization, order and life, on the other randomness, dissociation, chaos and death. And out of dissolution, I see new structures rising again—plants drawing nourishment from the decomposed remains of other plants, animals feeding on plants or other animals, mountains evolving out of the debris of older mountains leveled by erosion—a never-ending cycle of construction and destruction, growth and decay, life and death.

For over 40 years, within the limits of my modest means, I have studied the macrostructures of nature and found in them a ceaseless source of joy and inspiration. Look, for example, at the broken clamshell shown on the opposite page. Superficially seen, few things are lower than a broken clamshell, less valuable, less beautiful. Yet to me, this little derelict is a delight, precisely because it is broken—broken in a way that reveals its internal structure: smooth, crystalline inner layers followed by ribbed layers succeeded by longitudinal layers combine to form a structure which, for its purpose, is flawlessly designed and executed. How many man-made structures exist about which that can be said?

Similar discoveries and observations can be made wherever we look in nature. The way, say, a skeleton—any skeleton—is "engineered" comes close to being a marvel. Each bone is formed in accordance with its function, its shape a tangible expression of the stresses and strains to which it is subjected, the whole put together in a way that must arouse our deepest admiration because it combines strictest economy of means with a maximum of functional efficacy. The same can be said of cholla skeletons (p. 60) and the meshlike skeletons of sea cucumbers (p. 61), structures of which it is hard to believe that they organized themselves without intelligent guidance simply by following the "blueprint" encoded in the respective plant's or animal's genes. And the shells of mollusks (pp. 62–63), which many people consider mere blobs of animated slime, could serve as examples of perfect engineering in the curriculum of any technical teaching institute. Other examples of "perfect engineering" are feathers, which combine a maximum of strength with a minimum of weight while at the same time achieving an unsurpassed degree of thermal insulation; spiderwebs, the silk of which exceeds structural steel in tensile strength and flexibility; eggshells, which, by their form, achieve an almost unbelievable degree of resistance to crushing; the seeds of many plants and their ingenious devices for distribution; the incredibly "sophisticated" means many plants have developed to assure pollination. Studying these and other "technical" accomplishments of nature with an eye to exploitation through adaptation and utilization of their principles in order to carry the art of human engineering to new heights is a field that so far has hardly been touched.

Opposite: A broken clamshell reveals its internal structure.

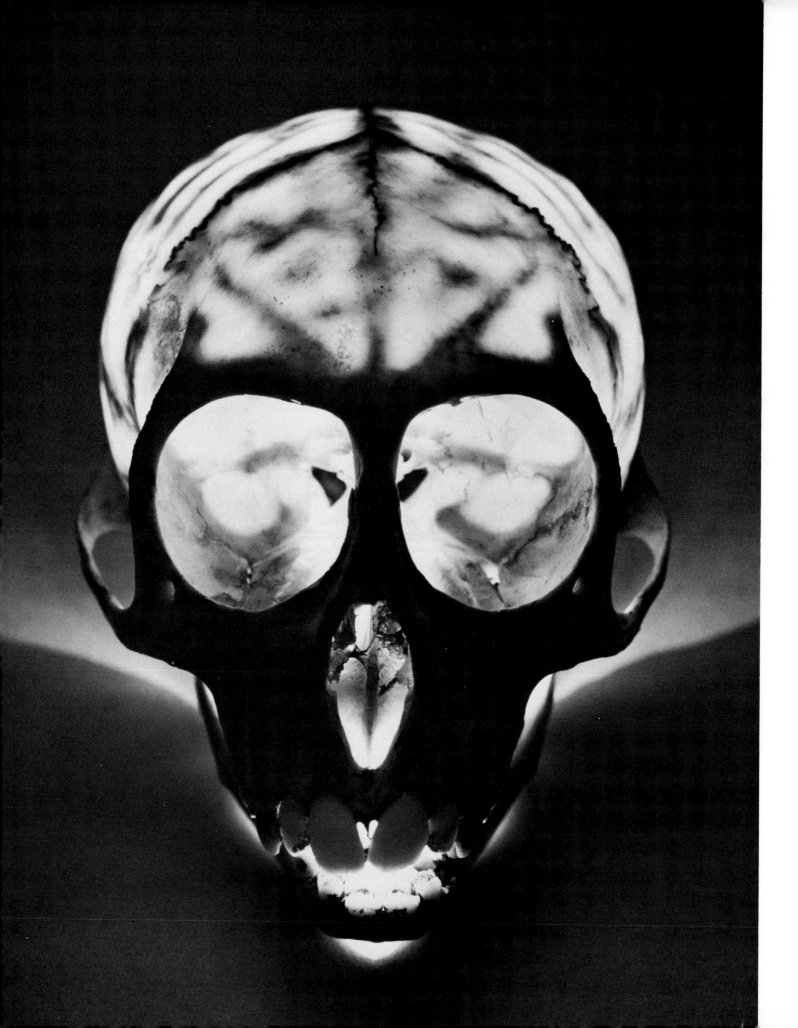

Above: The pelvis of a three-toed sloth. Designed as if in accordance with modern engineering theories, it utilizes the principle of the ring, the strongest yet lightest of all structural forms. Elimination of unnecessary bone material—the holes in the lateral plates—makes the skeleton of this tree-climbing animal even lighter. *Opposite:* Skull of a small monkey. The interior lighting, like X-ray photography, reveals how arched ridges reinforce the shell in strategic places, while bracing "beams"—zones where new bone is deposited as the shell expands in growth—strengthen the skull along the intrinsically weaker lines of juncture of the plates.

Above: The rib cage of a gorilla. *Opposite:* The pelvic complex of a bird. The study of skeletal structures is infinitely rewarding from the point of view of both the engineer and the artist because bones and their assemblies are not only functional to the highest degree but also beautiful. The rib cage encases heart and lungs—the body's most vital organs—in bony armor, articulated and yielding, yet tough and strong. The pelvic complex, a thin, shell-like structure reinforced by the fused bones of the spine and braced by struts like the keel of a ship for absolute rigidity, combines minimum weight with maximum strength and resistance to deformation.

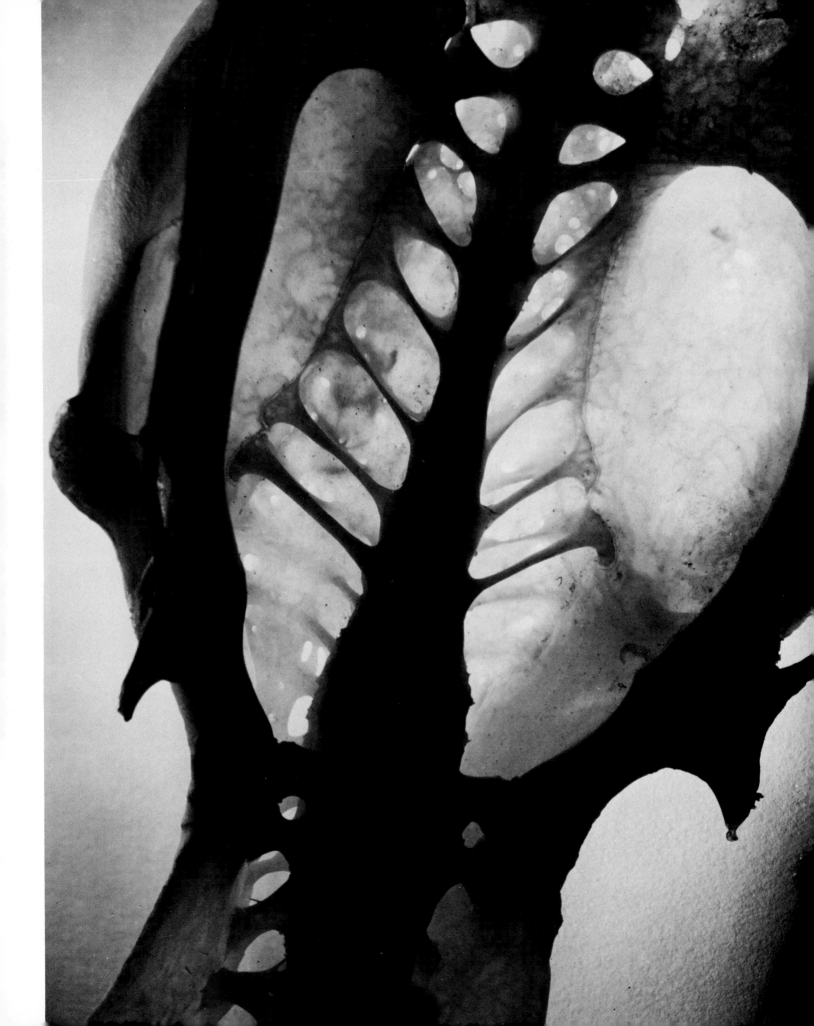

The hinge was not invented by man, nor was the ball-and-socket joint. Both were anticipated by nature, as proven by these photographs. *Above:* A human elbow joint shown in a multiple-exposure photograph. *Opposite:* The ball-and-socket joint of the hip. In life, of course, a perfect fit is insured by means of cartilaginous inserts and a lubrication system designed to last throughout life, the entire structure backed up by the ability to service itself and, if necessary, perform minor repairs.

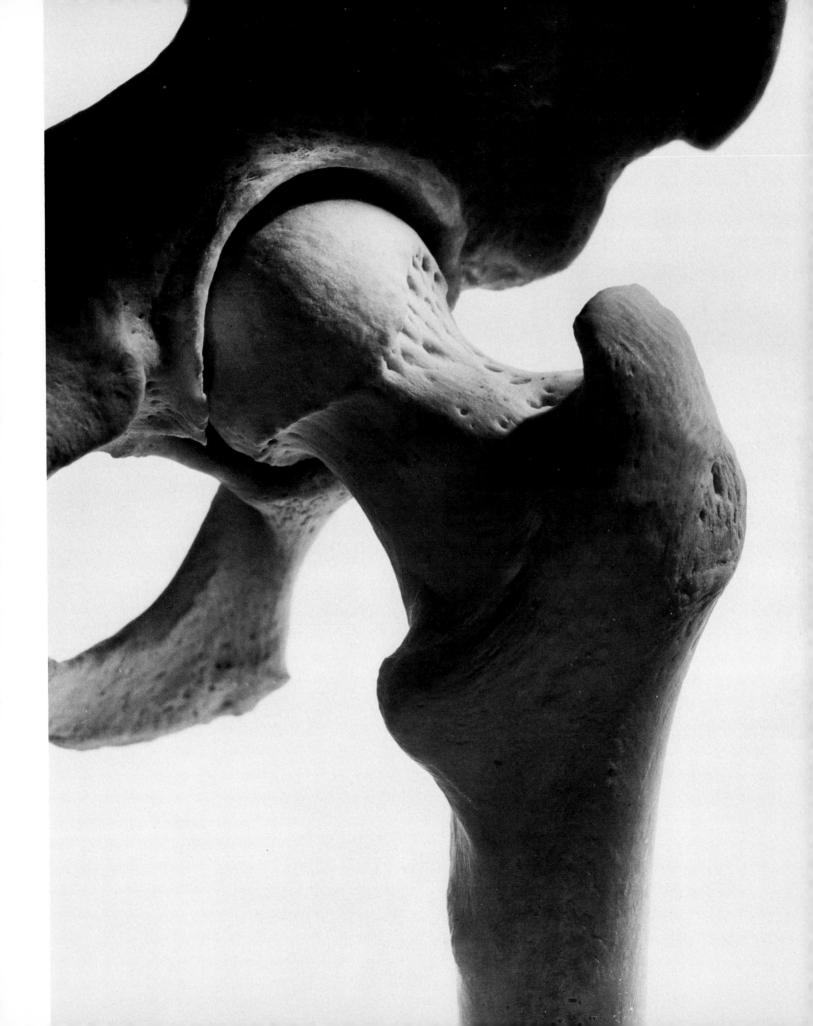

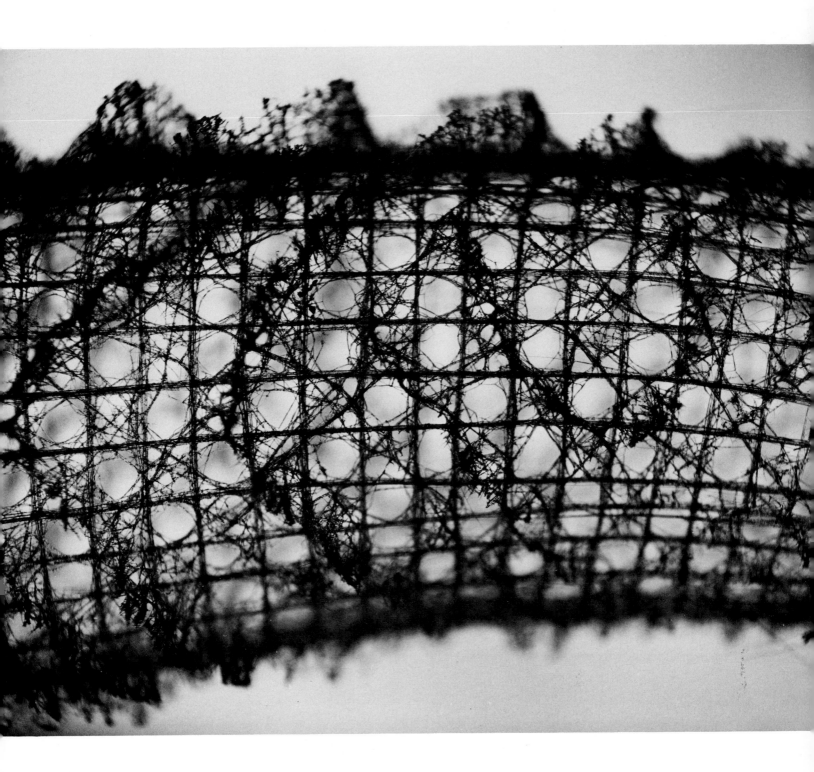

Above: The mesh-like internal skeleton of a sea cucumber, an echinoderm of the class *Holothuroidea. Opposite:* The skeleton of a cholla, a cactus of the genus *Opuntia.* In both cases, a tubular structure, perfectly designed to achieve a maximum of strength with a minimum expenditure of material, is used to provide support for its owner, rivaling, if not surpassing, all similar structures designed by man. Again, the identical principle is used by animal and plant.

Shell engineering. *Above:* A close-up of the aperture of a black-lined tun shell (*Tonna melanostoma* Jay) reveals the corrugation by means of which this mollusk increases the strength of its thin shell significantly, utilizing the same principle as that employed by man in the manufacture of corrugated cardboard and tin. Again, the shell "discovered" this principle first. *Opposite:* An opening cut into the shell of a West Indian chank (*Turbinella angulatum* Lightfoot) reveals its structural beauty. That this gleaming, ivory-like helix—the columella—is the work of a "slimy" mollusk is hard to believe. The purpose of the corrugation is to increase the surface of the columella, thereby providing a maximum of attachment for the body of the snail.

I see in structures like these proof that nothing in nature is insignificant, that applying the term "insignificant" to any object of nature is a sign of either ignorance or stupidity, and that the more we study the apparently insignificant aspects of nature, the more we are likely to learn, to gain in understanding and to appreciate the wonders of our world.

Design

The word "design" has many connotations. To me, it primarily suggests two concepts: order and beauty. Order implies clarity, simplicity and function; beauty implies sense-appeal. Perhaps I am prejudiced, but I find these qualities much more often in objects of nature than in the works of man. In nature, nothing is ugly, although many of her creations are unfamiliar to many people—and unfamiliarity, particularly in conjunction with low intelligence or lack of education, easily arouses suspicion, revulsion, hate and fear. Nor is there anything meaningless, inefficient or nonfunctional in nature, while badly functioning and senseless man-made creations abound.

The natural designs shown on the following pages were chosen for several reasons. Some I picked for their decorative values—for example, the fortuitous patterns created by paper wasps (pp. 66–67) and by the textures of sand or stone (pp. 68–69 and 90–91). A comparison with modern abstract art suggests itself: in both cases, the effect on the viewer depends not so much on the subject of the picture as such (here wasp-nest material, sand or stone) as on what the observer of the photograph is able to see in it. It is his imagination—his contribution—that determines the value of such pictures.

I selected other subjects with the aim of documenting the creative or "imaginative" force in nature. By showing different designs (different "solutions") for, say, trees (pp. 70–71), leaves (pp. 72–73), insect wings (p. 76) or devices for the distribution of seeds by wind (pp. 78–79), I wanted to show that, in most instances, a basic problem can be solved in different ways, each variant depending on, and carefully adapted to, a specific set of conditions. A parallel, involving such man-made objects as, for example, automobiles, spoons or screwdrivers, could easily be drawn: each of these objects exists in a great variety of different designs, all of which, however, have the same basic purpose.

And then there are designs created by specific, function-related arrangements of objects of nature, as in the case of leaf mosaics (pp. 86–87), the purpose of which is to assure each individual leaf of a maximum exposure to light without impairing the efficacy of the others by casting a shadow on them. The resulting designs not only are admirable from a purely functional point of view but also form aesthetically pleasing patterns which, say, a textile designer might incorporate almost unchanged into his creations.

Approached in this spirit, natural designs can become a virtually inexhaustible source of creative inspiration. This, of course, is nothing new, as proven by innumerable flower and leaf designs on fabrics, dinnerware, painted furniture, and so on. But flowers and leaves are not the only designs suitable to exploitation, nor is a literal adaptation always the best. Modification and stylization can increase the number of patterns a thousandfold besides leading to more interesting designs, different, new, never before seen . . .

The stunning rosette on the opposite page is not the inspired design for a window in a great cathedral, but the flower-supporting structure of Queen Anne's lace, one of the most common of all wildflowers in my part of Connecticut.

Two close-ups of the paperlike material that forms the wall of a nest of white-faced hornets. Differences in color are due to differences in the type of wood the insects used to manufacture the pulp for the construction of their nest. Contemplating designs like these always makes me wonder to what degree nonrepresentational modern painting is indebted to nature.

Above: Texture of sand dunes in California's Death Valley. The area shown is approximately ten feet wide. *Opposite:* A ventifact—a sandblasted stone—from Death Valley. Both surface structures are the result of wind action which, in the first case, ripple-marked the sand and, in the second example, eroded the stone surface by selectively removing the softer particles first, an effect that may have been aided by leaching. In either case, the result is a strongly organized pattern I find aesthetically attractive.

70

Each species of animal or plant has its own design—a collection of unique characteristics that set it apart from all the others. This design permeates the entire organism to such an extent that an expert can recognize and name correctly, say, a tree, even in winter, despite the absence of flowers and leaves.

The photograph at the top of the opposite page shows a white oak in Maryland; the one above, a sugar maple in Connecticut. The differences in the design of these two trees is as evident in their growth pattern as it is in the form of their leaves.

At bottom of the opposite page is an ornamentally pruned or pollarded sycamore in France—man's design forcibly superimposed on that of nature.

SWEET BIRCH

TULIP-Tree

Chestnut OAK

Horsechestnut

SUGAR MAPLE

RED OAK

TULIPTREE

Shagb. Hickory
(leaven NOT apparent)

BLACK LOCUST

GINKGO

MULBERRY

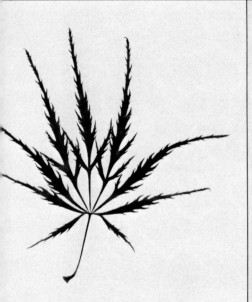

SASSAFRAS

MULBERRY

ASPEN

Two pages from my photographic sketchbook. Leaves from different species of trees testify to the boundless inventiveness of nature, which has varied one basic design to an infinite degree—taking into consideration the fact that probably no two leaves, even from the same tree, are ever exactly alike.

Marvel at the beauty of the individual designs, each attractive in its own way: edges smooth or wavy, serrated; leaves roundish, pinnately or palmately lobed, symmetrical or asymmetrical, pointed or indented at the tip, surfaces smooth or rough . . . Why, one wonders, this infinite variety instead of only one form for all?

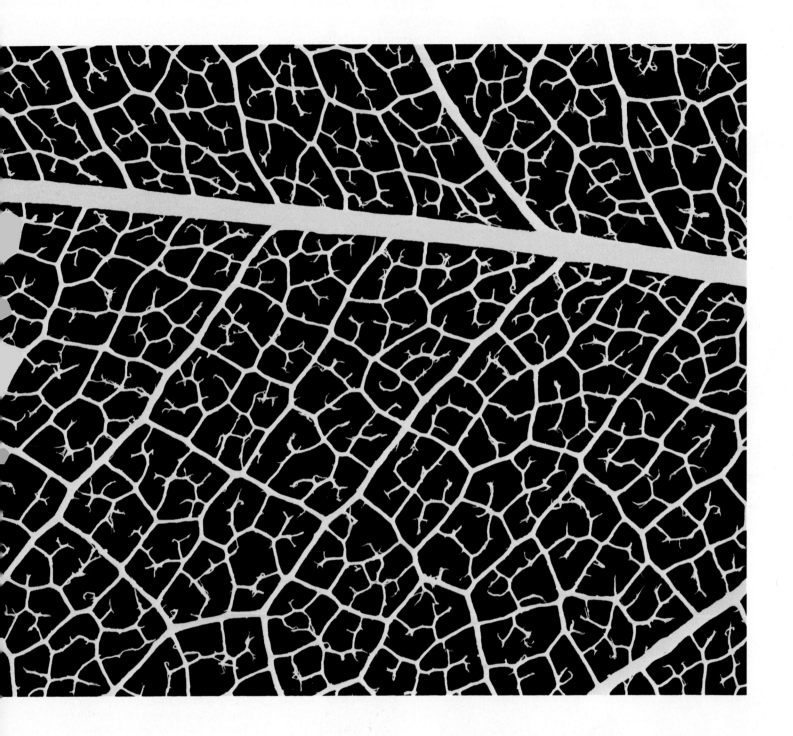

A closer look at leaves reveals the intricacy of their designs. *Above:* A greatly enlarged view of a section of a leaf from which everything but the veins has been removed by chemical treatment. It shows the regularity with which the system of veins covers the entire leaf in such a way that no point is farther removed from the distributing network than any other. *Opposite:* The photograph of a decaying chestnut oak leaf reveals the overall design of its veins.

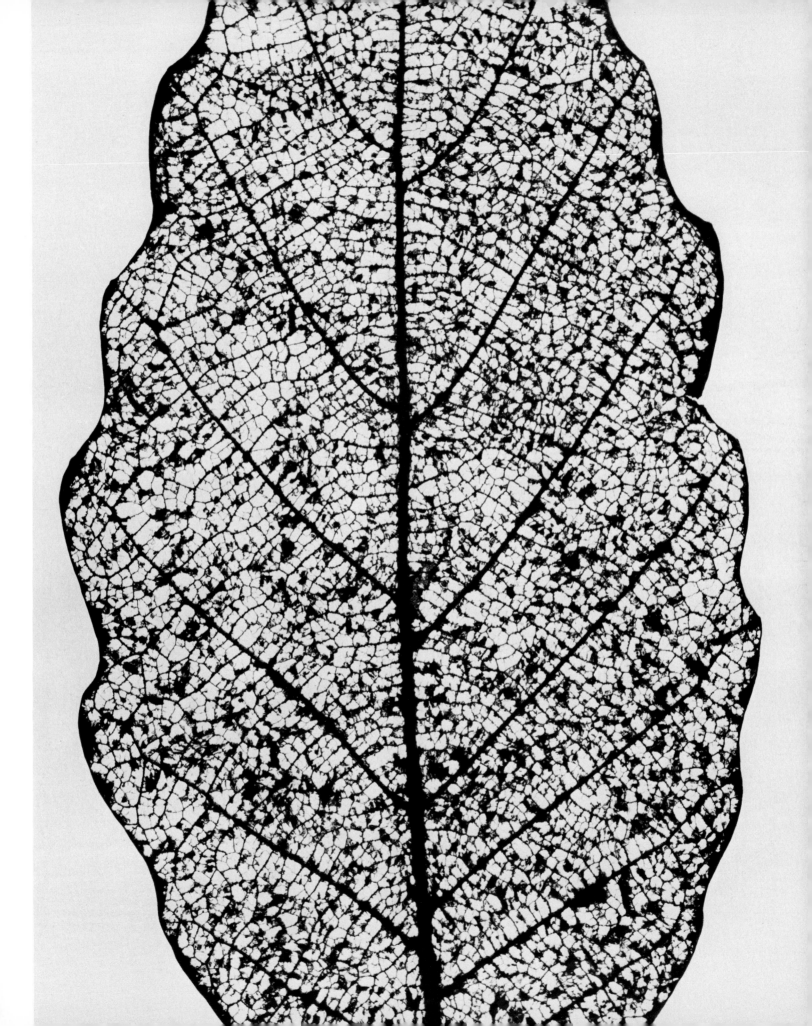

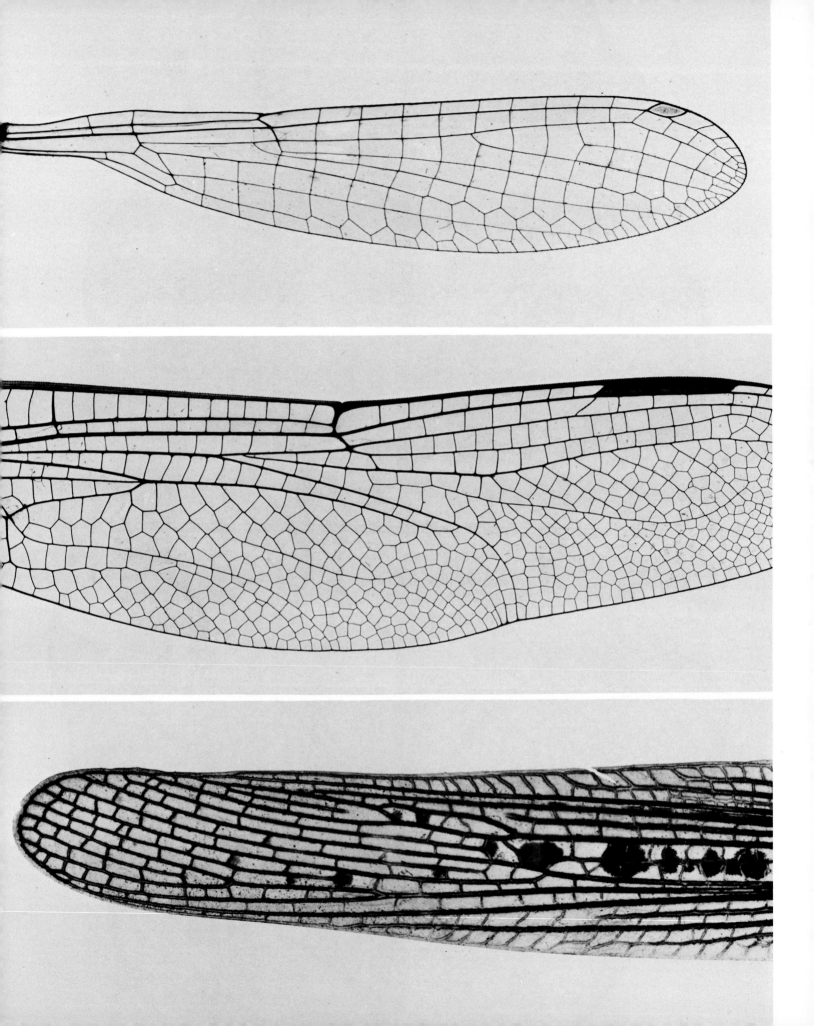

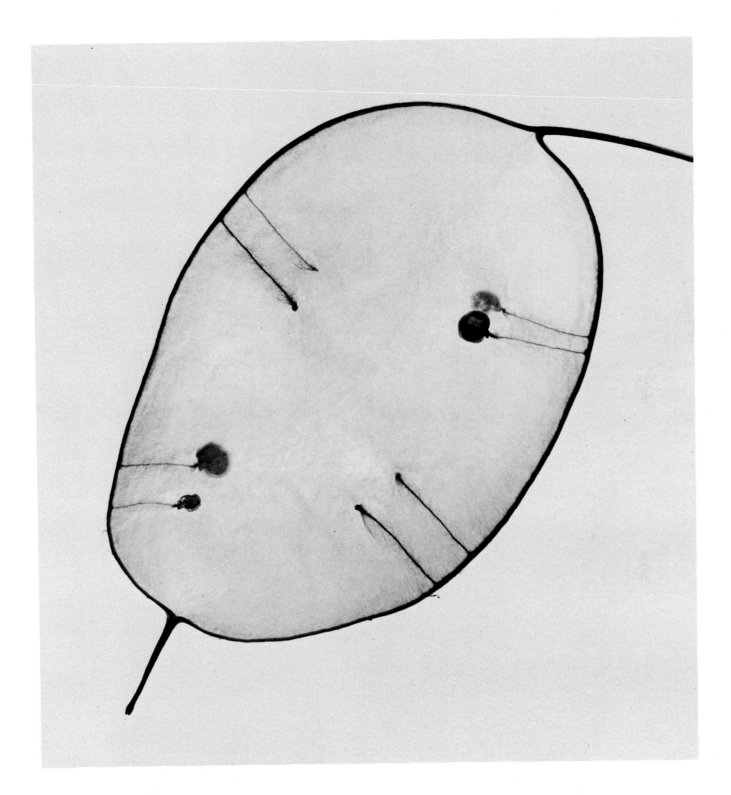

The problem: how to stiffen a membrane. *Opposite:* Wings from different insects. *Above:* The dividing membrane of a silver-dollar seed capsule. The design of the insect wings embodies the principle of stiffening by branching ribs; the seed membrane employs a tension ring, analogous to the rim of a banjo or tambourine.

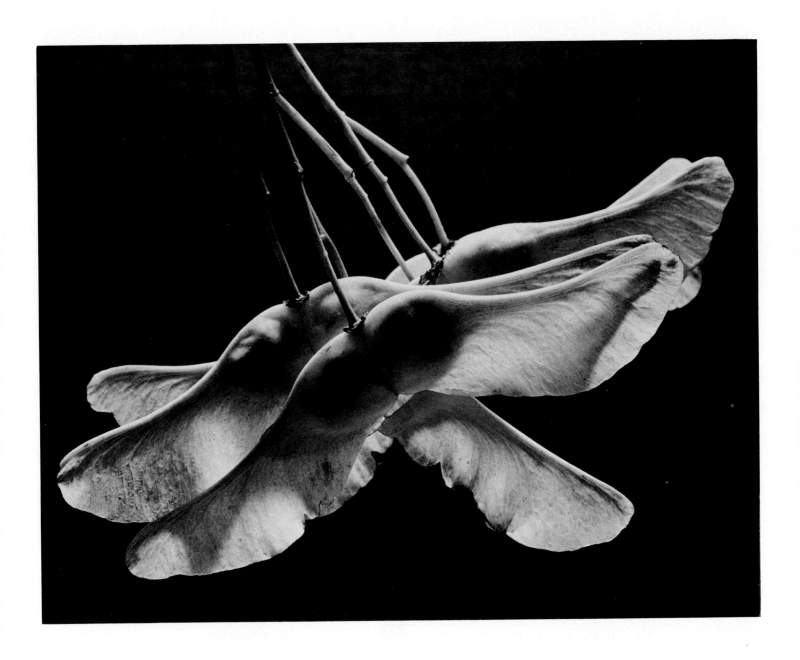

To assure maximum dispersal, seeds employ some of the most ingenious devices in nature. Illustrated here are two forms designed for aerial distribution. *Above:* The propeller-driven seeds of maple. *Opposite:* Descending milkweed seeds strike the ground like falling bombs.

Designs for plant mobility through seed dispersal. *Above:* Dandelion seeds. *Opposite:* Sycamore seeds. Seeds are among nature's most diversified, ingenious and thought-provoking creations. Some hook to the coats of animals and fall away as the animals rove. Others are dispersed by birds who feed upon fruit but eliminate the indigestible seeds. Still others fall to closer ground, shot to distances of several yards when the drying seed pods split with a snap. Some travel with ocean currents and tides, remaining buoyant for months, retaining power to germinate and grow in distant island soils. But the greatest number travel with the wind, gliding on gossamer parachutes like the dandelion seeds; spinning in spiral flight and descent on miniature propeller forms, like the maple seeds; or whirling in a rolling race with prairie winds to shake from the parent husk, like the seeds of the tumbleweed.

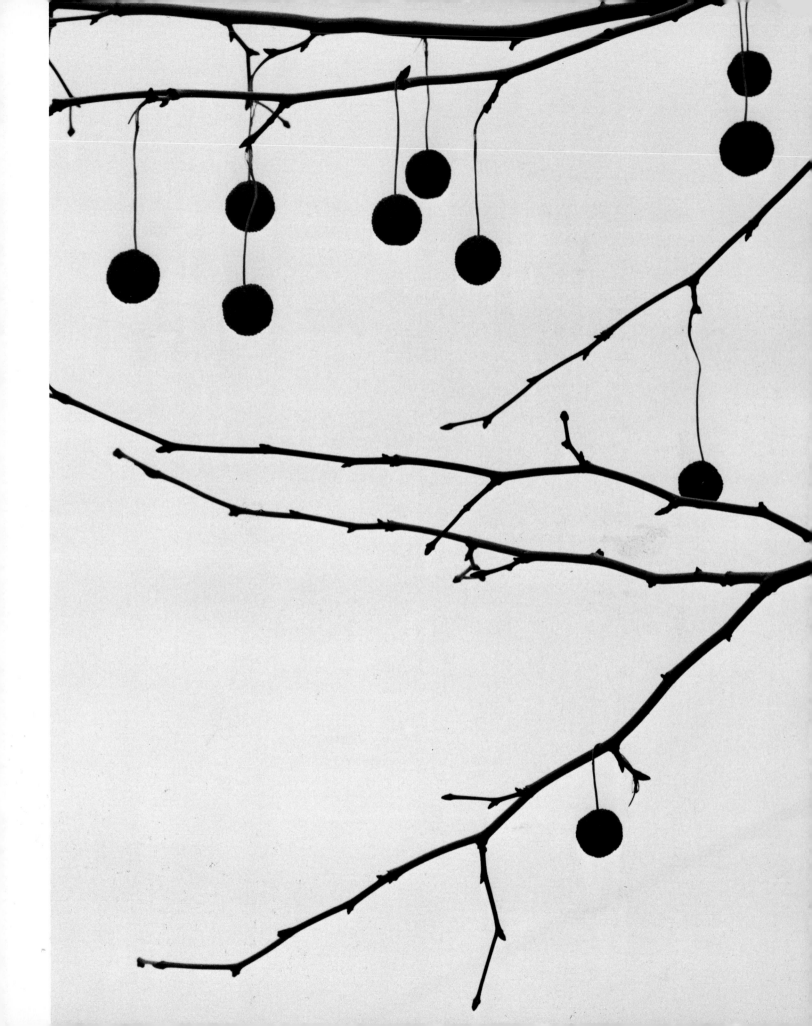

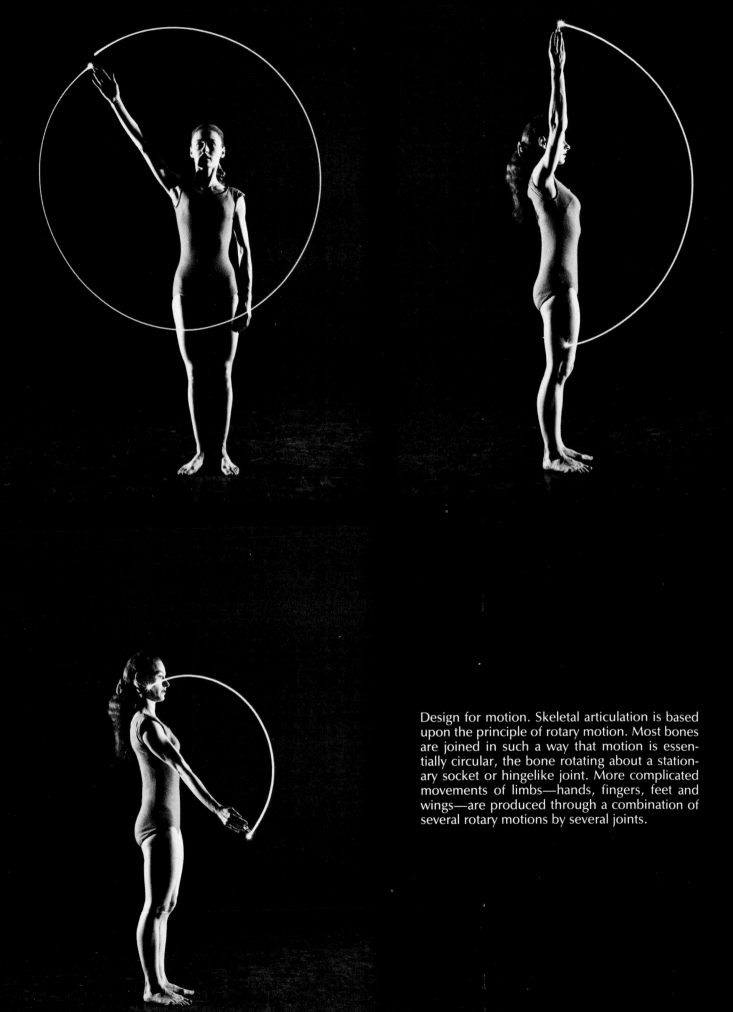

Design for motion. Skeletal articulation is based upon the principle of rotary motion. Most bones are joined in such a way that motion is essentially circular, the bone rotating about a stationary socket or hingelike joint. More complicated movements of limbs—hands, fingers, feet and wings—are produced through a combination of several rotary motions by several joints.

The photographs on this spread illustrate the principal motions of the human body with the aid of small, battery-fed flashlight lamps attached to the hand, foot and shoulder of a dancer. The center of each motion is a major joint—the shoulder, the elbow, the knee, the hip. The movements were taken by time exposure in the dark; the dancer was flashed at the end of the motion.

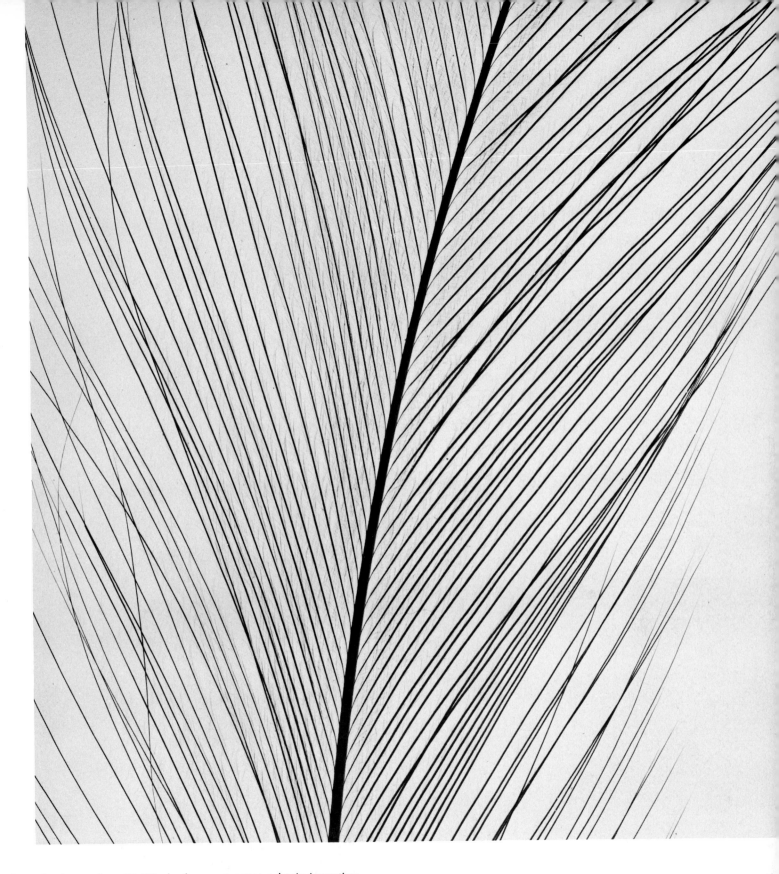

Like leaves (pp. 72–73), feathers represent a basic invention which nature has modified in design to an almost infinite degree—each type adapted to serve most perfectly a specific purpose which may vary from strictly functional to entirely ornamental. Two examples, each beautiful in its own way, are shown on this spread.

Above: Vine of a wild grape. *Opposite:* Vine of a wild rose. Two variations on a basic design of nature—the leaf mosaic—which are both functional and beautiful. Functional because they represent leaf arrangements that give each leaf a maximum of exposure to light. Beautiful because almost any pattern consisting of a repetition of similar elements ipso facto creates an aesthetically satisfying design.

Leaf mosaics. *Above:* Sumach, a tree of the genus *Rhus. Opposite:* Flowering dogwood. Even in arrangements as complex as these, leaves naturally position themselves in growth in such a way that overlapping—with accompanying shading of neighboring leaves—is avoided to an amazingly high degree.

Landscapes in stone? No—only chance patterns created by random penetration of extraneous material into certain types of rocks. But the receptive eye sees in these patterns a Chinese landscape *(above)* and the crags and cloud-filled valleys of a mountain range *(opposite)*. Unscientific? Yes, definitely. Silly? Perhaps—but like so many silly things, enjoyable and possibly

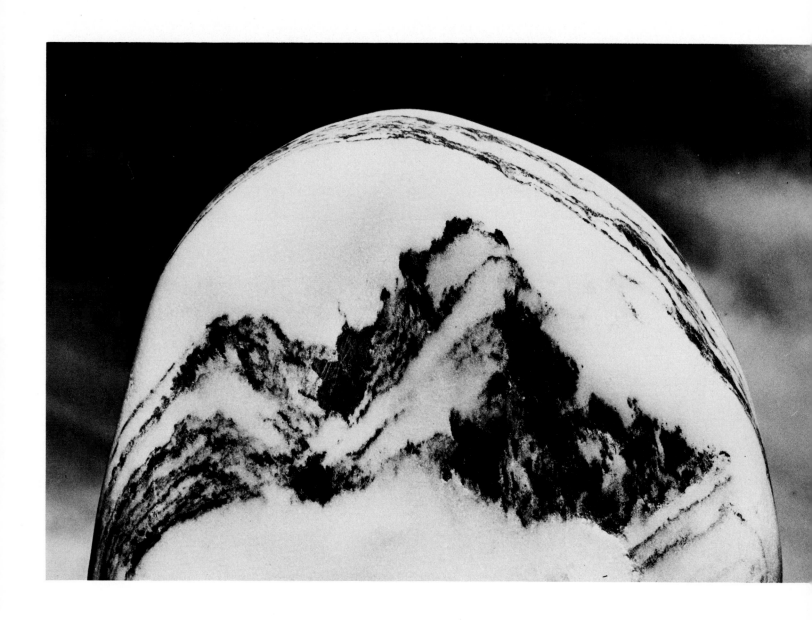

stimulating, turning the mind to other, more serious thoughts
. . . China and Chinese pen-and-ink drawings, rock-strewn
mountain slopes, the Himalayas, Mt. Everest, highest peak in
the world, heights both in reality and of the mind, infinity,
eternity, why am I here on Earth . . .

Above: Close-up of a flat-ground slab of sandstone. *Opposite:* Detail of a reed. One a capricious design of nature, the other a highly organized structure, both are capable of arousing a host of . . . related? . . . unrelated? . . . images in a receptive mind. I see in the sandstone a sunset and think of the work of Van Gogh and southern France, while the reed makes me think of classic columns, Greece and Rome, and all kinds of tubular, technical as well as sculptural designs. Also of marshes and the scratchy but lovable song of redwings, of Stockholm, where I took this photograph, of the early days of my marriage when I took it, and from there on of an endless progression of various aspects of life. There just is no end to the stimulating effects objects of nature can have on an open mind.

Similarities

In the course of my explorations of the structural forms of nature I have found again and again that completely unrelated objects can have a perplexing similarity. As shown on the following pages, dendrites—patterns created by mineralized solutions that penetrated into cracks in rocks, where they dried and crystallized—"grow" like trees *(opposite)*; designs formed by cracks in drying mud and the venation in leaves are identical down to the last detail and both, in turn, have an uncanny resemblance to the markings on giraffes as well as the surface configurations of certain types of chert, a mineral (pp. 96–99). And then there is that astonishing structural similarity between insect wings and leaves (pp. 100–101), or between the defensive thorns of certain plants, fishes and shells (pp. 102–103). Grasses and feathers are designed in accordance with the same basic plan (pp. 104–105), palm fronds and frost on a windowpane grow following the same design (pp. 106–107), and so on. What does all this mean?

Specialists with whom I discussed these phenomena assured me that all such similarities are either entirely by chance or the result of convergent adaptation—unrelated species of plants or animals reacting to the same stimulus with the same response: in the case of defensive requirements they developed thorns. Here, then, we have the first indication, if not proof, of a basic natural "law" that applies to all living things, regardless whether animals or plants. But I believe there are other basic "laws," such as, for example, the principle of surface tension that rules the formation of cracks in surfaces and may apply equally to drying mud, venation in insect wings or leaves, pattern formation in giraffe skin, or surface cracks on chert. Insect wings may resemble leaves because, in both cases, a living membrane had to be stiffened and at the same time supplied with ducts for solutions; identical problems led to identical answers, although, in one case, the "inventor" was an animal and in the other case a plant. And by the same reasoning we can explain the structural similarities between grasses and feathers: the mechanical demands are the same in both cases; hence, similar solutions with subsequent similarity in appearance. But how does one explain the similarity between, for example, the growth patterns of palm fronds, feathers and ice crystals on a windowpane?

To me, contemplation of such problems is an extraordinarily stimulating and rewarding activity. Discovering similarities between totally unrelated objects and phenomena of nature provides me with the proof I need to confirm my belief that connections exist between even the most unlikely and apparently unrelated things; that the laws of nature are few and universal, applying to all creatures which therefore have equal rights to exist; that the ways of nature are marvelous beyond belief, mysterious, unfathomable; and that I, a humble yet exalted human being, related to the animals and plants, made of the same stuff as the earth and the stars, am part of the universe.

What has all this to do with art? A good deal—on two different levels. First, studying the ways in which nature has "engineered" her creations can have practical rewards in regard to human engineering for reasons already given in the Foreword. But beyond such pragmatic considerations, anything that stimulates the mind also stimulates creativity—and creativity is the basis of all forms of art. Nature, man and art are linked inextricably.

Sugar maple in winter and a dendrite—the product of mineralized solutions infiltrating and crystallizing in cracks in stone. The similarity between these two structures, although allegedly fortuitous, is thought-provoking.

95

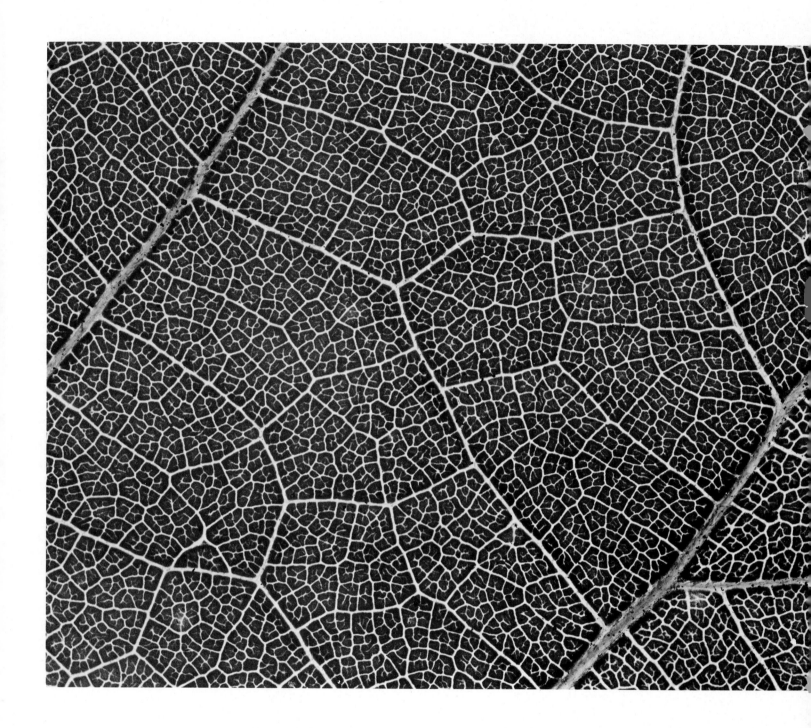

Above: Venation in a leaf. *Opposite:* Cracked mud at the bottom of a playa, a shallow desert lake, here dry. I find it fascinating how similar those polygonal patterns are to each other as well as to those on the following two pages. The mud cracks are caused by surface tension. Could the same principle apply also to leaves? Is it possible that surface tension "splits" the leaf material during growth, that cracklike zones of weakness develop, and that veins take the opportunity to occupy these ready-made spaces.

Above: Giraffe. *Opposite:* Snakeskin chert, a mineral. Once more, two objects as different as an animal and a stone exhibit the same surface patterns, identical to the last detail, including the pentagonal forms and the beginnings of secondary "cracks." Coincidence? Perhaps, but I doubt it. In the stone, the cracks are caused by surface tension; how the pattern of the giraffe evolved is open to speculation.

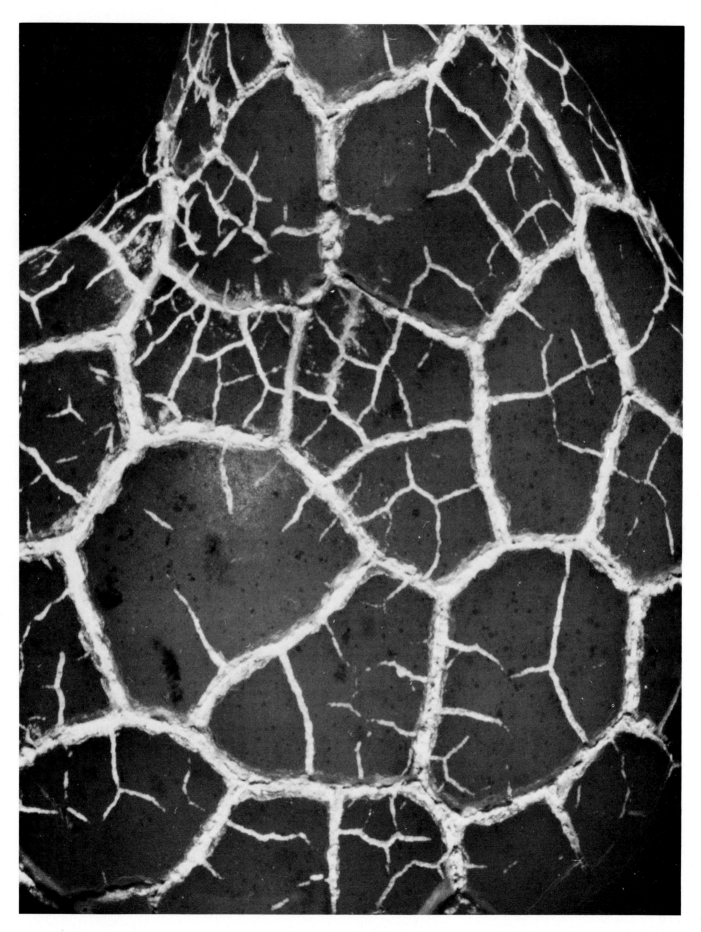

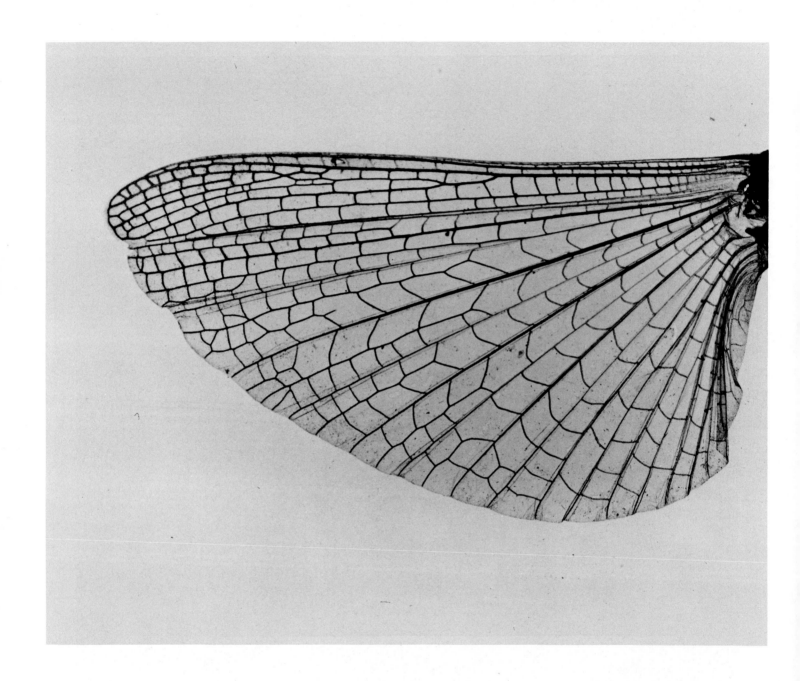

Above: Hind wing of a grasshopper. *Opposite:* Venation in a leaf, magnified approximately 10× linear. The resemblance in design is unmistakable, the principle underlying both structures the same: a membrane had to be stiffened and at the same time supplied with ducts for solutions which, in the case of the grasshopper, subsequently hardened, further reinforcing the wing. Insect and plant made use of the same structural design.

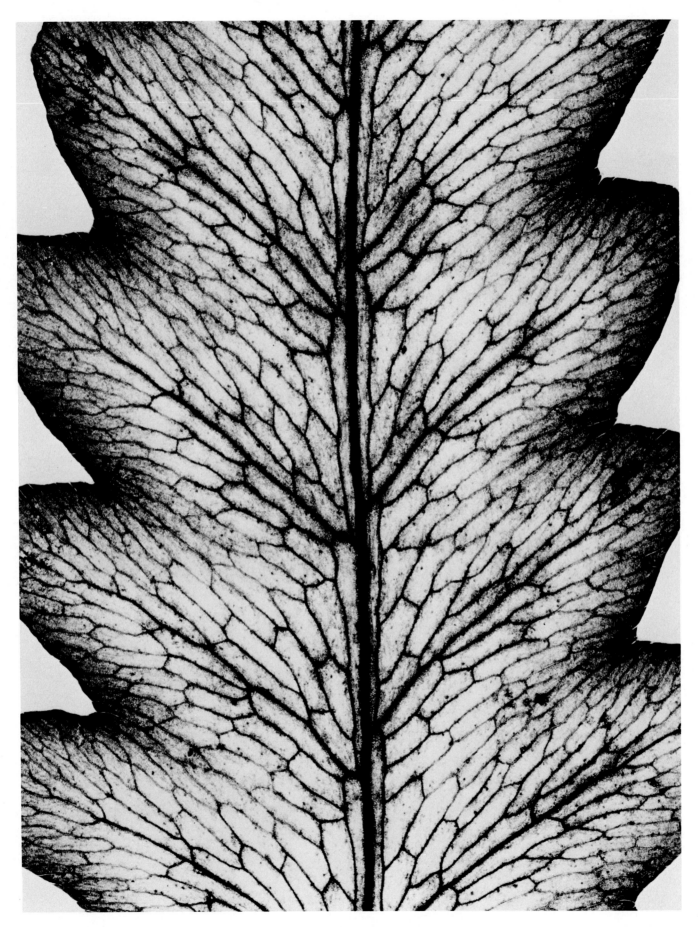

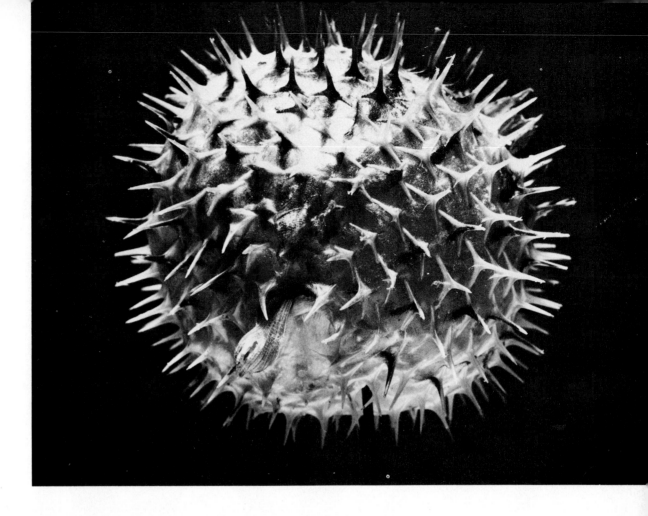

Opposite: Thorns of a rose. *Above:* Spines of a blowfish. *Left:* Spines of a prickly cockle shell (*Acanthocardia aculeata* Linné). Identical defensive requirements result in identical defensive means—thorns—regardless whether the "inventor" is a plant, a fish or a shell: a typical example of convergent adaptation.

Above: Feathers. *Opposite:* Grasses in seed. Another one of those "coincidental" design similarities in nature, this time between grasses and feathers. Surprising, isn't it, how decorative strictly functional forms can be? Perhaps there is a lesson for industrial designers who all too often corrupt the functional creations of the engineer.

Above: Frost pattern on a windowpane. *Opposite:* A coconut palm. The similarity in design is striking—and thought-provoking. Science calls it chance. But considering the paucity of our knowledge of the more subtle phenomena of nature, I am inclined to doubt this. Perhaps, some day, we will know . . .

Above: Part of the root system of a fallen beech. *Opposite:* Pollarded sycamore in France. Many modern sculptures seem to have been inspired by natural forms like these. Whereas the root might give rise to a constructivist creation, the tortured branches of the sycamore look like goblins holding bunches of flowers in widespread hands.

Symmetry

Symmetry represents a very high degree of order and manifests itself in many forms, from classic temples to butterflies. In man-made works, symmetry is common and easily achieved. But in objects of nature it seems an almost miraculous accomplishment: how does one side of a living growing organism —no matter whether animal or plant—"know" what the other side is doing so that it can keep up with it and mirror it in every respect?

The human body is, at least externally, virtually symmetrical: we have two eyes, two ears, two arms, two legs, and so on, the parts on one side mirroring those on the other. But what and where is the mechanism or coordinator which prevents one side from developing differently from the other? Science tells me that such aspects of growth are genetically fixed characteristics of their possessors, which is doubtless true; but it really doesn't "explain" anything and leaves the process of growth as miraculous as ever.

Symmetry manifests itself in two forms: bilateral and radial. Examples of bilateral symmetry in nature are mammals, birds, fishes, insects, orchids, the flowers of the catalpa tree, many leaves, and so on. Examples of radial symmetry are starfish, sea anemones, sea urchins, radiolarians and flowers such as daisies, tulips, dandelions and many more.

Symmetrical forms are intrinsically decorative, radial-symmetrical ones perhaps even more so than bilateral forms. They have a quiet dignity, are symbols of planning and order. This is the point I want to make with the photographs in this and the following chapter: there is order in nature, in the universe—structure, coordination, cohesion and unity, an overall design in which all parts fit together and depend on one another as in a giant puzzle. Contemplating the symmetrical forms of nature is to me a form of meditation, promoting peace of mind.

Swallowtail. Marvel at the fidelity with which one side of the ornamental pattern on a butterfly's wing is mirrored in the other side, down to the last detail. To me, this is an almost miraculous accomplishment of nature, for how does one side "know" what the other one is doing so each can match the other?

Above: Tulip-tree leaf. *Opposite:* Stones shaped and polished by the surf. The perfection and beauty of simple natural forms . . .

Above: Starfish. *Opposite:* Daisy. Examples of radial symmetry in nature which have inspired countless man-made ornaments and decorative designs. What kind of mechanism rules the growth of these shapes—a mechanism that can count and divide a circle into a given number of equal parts? It's all in the genes, they say . . . but what, precisely, does that mean?

Spirals

The spiral is one of nature's basic design forms. We find it in structures as different as Crick and Watson's "double helix"—the DNA molecule, the tentacles of plants, the shells of mollusks, the arrangement of seeds in sunflowers, the vortices in water and air, and the swirling star clouds of spiral galaxies.

In nature, spirals occur in two forms: as single spirals, and in the form of two integrated sets of spirals curving clockwise and counterclockwise, respectively, like opposite-directed pinwheels. Representatives of the first kind are nautilus shells and snails (pp. 122–123), the tentacles of vines and the egg cases of whelks (pp. 118–121). The second kind forms part of the design of many plants (pp. 124–127). The seeds of sunflowers, the scales of pinecones, the bumps on pineapples, the florets of daisies and Queen Anne's lace, and the spines of certain cacti, for example, are arranged in the form of two sets of opposing spirals integrated in a strict geometric order. This form of organization is in itself remarkable. But what makes it truly amazing is the fact that the number of spirals in each set is not identical, but invariably coincides with two adjacent numbers of the Fibonacci sequence. This is the mathematical progression 1, 1, 2, 3, 5, 8, 13, 21, 34, 55, 89, and so on, each term being the sum of the two terms immediately preceding. Now, the number of spirals in pinecones, pineapples, Queen Anne's lace and certain cacti is 8 and 13, in other cacti 13 and 21, in most daisies 21 and 34, and in sunflowers 55 and 89—the same ratios as those of two adjacent Fibonacci numbers. Why this is so is unknown.

Again the reader might ask: what has all this to do with art? The answer is more surprising than perhaps anything said so far because it reveals another startling connection between nature and art, specifically, between the Fibonacci numbers (which, as shown in this chapter, are an integral aspect of some of nature's designs) and the Golden Section or Golden Mean—the artist's famous canon of beauty which decrees that, aesthetically, the most pleasing ratio between two portions of a line, or between the two dimensions of a plane figure, is achieved if the lesser of the two is to the greater as the greater is to the sum of both—a ratio of approximately 0.616 to 1.000. Now, the ratio between the Fibonacci numbers 2 and 3 is 0.666 to 1.000—a reasonable approximation —but the ratio between 55 and 89 is already 0.6179 to 1.000—a value considerably closer to the ratio of the Golden Section than the ratio of 2 to 3. But what is even more surprising is the fact that the higher the value of the pair of Fibonacci numbers is, the closer their ratio approaches that of the Golden Section, which it would finally match in the ideal case of an infinitely high Fibonacci number pair. Nature designing some of its creations in strict adherence to man's most cherished beauty code in art—something to think about . . . for the next ten minutes . . . or the next ten years . . .

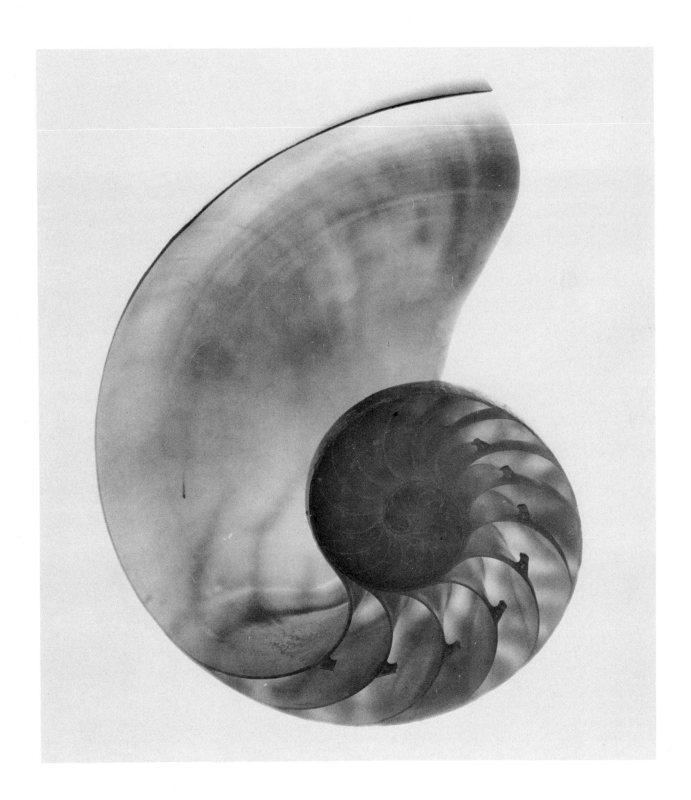

Shell of a chambered nautilus, a mollusk. This is one of nature's most amazing creations—a shell constructed along the lines of the most beautiful and sophisticated of all mathematical curves, a logarithmic spiral. But what makes this kind of spiral even more remarkable is that it is related, in a way too complex to go into here, to the Fibonacci numbers and the Golden Section discussed on the opposite page. There seems to be no end to nature's surprises . . .

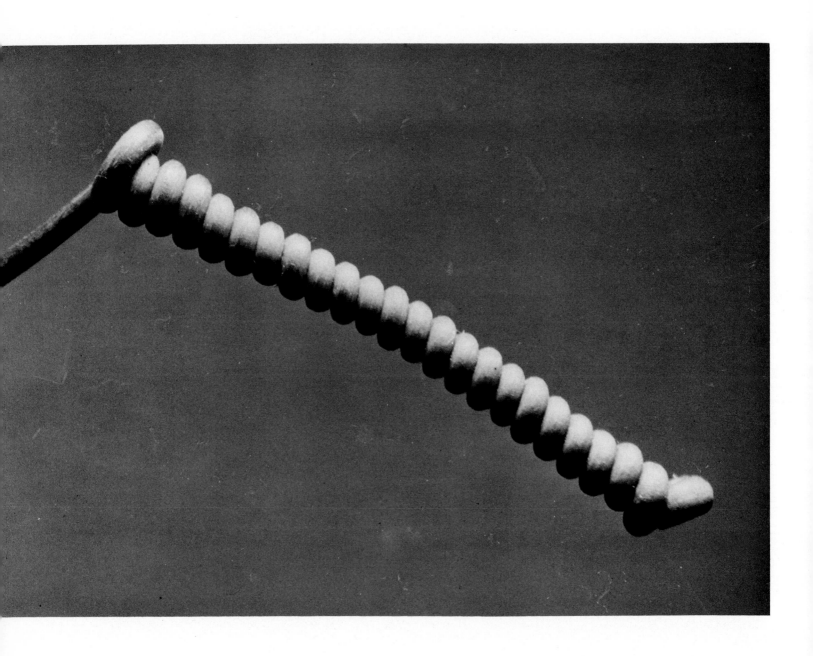

Above: Tentacle of a passion flower. Its tightly coiled spiral evokes the latent power of a steel spring. *Opposite:* Detail of a passion-flower plant, its coiled tentacle ready to reach out and anchor the vine securely to the nearest hold. Incidentally, its spiral form is identical with that of the coiled proboscis of butterflies and moths—another "coincidence" in nature.

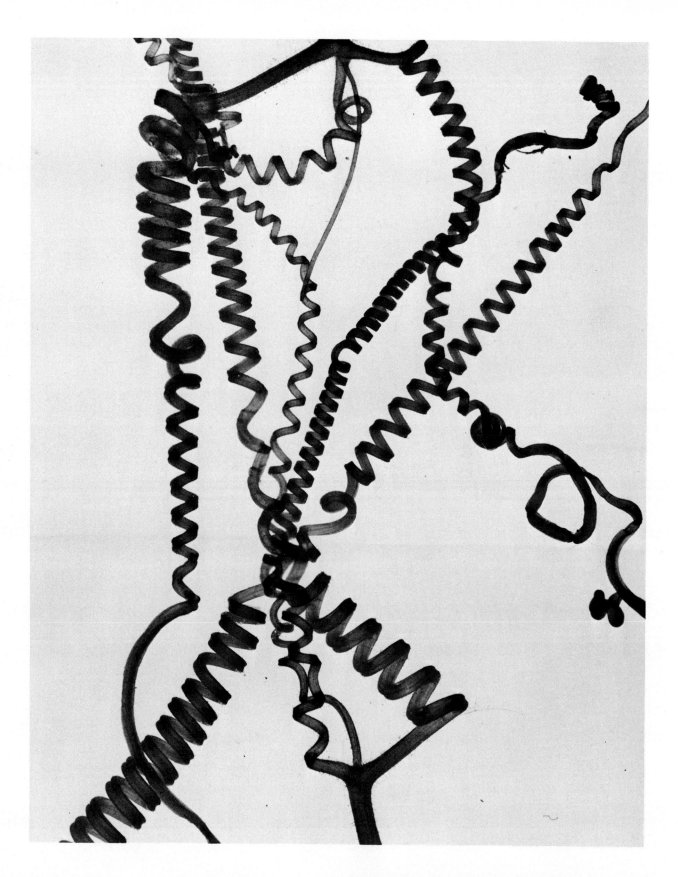

Above: The tentacles of a wild Connecticut grapevine form an abstract design. *Opposite:* The twisted strand of egg cases of a whelk, a large marine snail, repeats the double helix of the DNA molecule, one of nature's basic building elements.

Above: Close-up of the central part of a sundial shell (*Architectonica perspectivum* Linné), a perfect spiral minutely executed by a snail—a gastropod, a "mere mollusk" . . . *Opposite:* Detail of the sectioned shell of a chambered nautilus, a cephalopod, a member of a highly specialized group of mollusks. This time the shell is constructed in accordance with a logarithmic or equilateral spiral; if radii were drawn from the center of the shell, they would always intersect the spiral at identical angles. The question is: should we consider the fact that "snails" can construct their shells on the basis of sophisticated mathematical formulas as still another "coincidence"—or does it point to the existence of universal principles in nature?

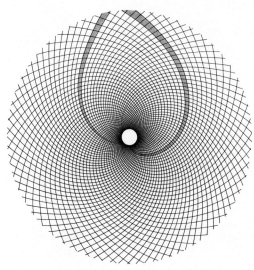

Sunflower with 55 counterclockwise and 89 clockwise spirals

The seeds in sunflowers *(above)* and the scales in pinecones *(opposite)* are arranged in the form of two sets of spirals curving clockwise and counterclockwise, respectively, like opposite-directed pinwheels. Mathematically precise, each set always contains a specific number of spirals that is typical for the respective species. The same design of opposing spirals also occurs in pineapples, certain cacti, Queen Anne's lace, daisies and other plants. Why this is so is not known.

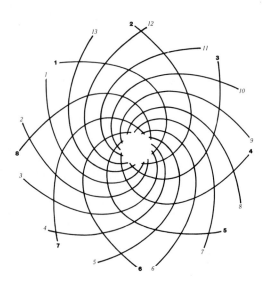

What makes this spiral design particularly thought-provoking is the fact that the number of spirals in each set invariably coincides with two adjacent numbers from a mathematical progression known as the Fibonacci sequence: 1, 1, 2, 3, 5, 8, 13, 21, 34, 55, 89 . . . as already explained on page 116. Now, the number of spirals is 8 and 13 in pinecones, pineapples, certain cacti and Queen Anne's lace; it is 13 and 21 in many other cacti, 21 and 34 in most daisies, and 34 and 55 (or, in larger flowers, 55 and 89) in sunflowers.

Pineapples *(opposite)* and certain species of cacti *(above)* are structured in accordance with the Fibonacci numbers, and I wonder: what is the connection between plants—which cannot "think," whose organization and manner of growth is genetically fixed—and mathematics? And are there other, similarly unexpected connections in nature which so far have escaped detection?

Ornamentation

The purpose of ornamentation is to improve the look of things. Man is an inveterate ornamenter, as proven not only by many of his artifacts, but also by his often compulsive tendency to decorate. Most people cannot see a plain wall or other surface without experiencing an almost irresistible urge to "beautify" it (or deface it with graffiti), superimposing a geometric arrangement, a floral pattern, a colorful design, filling walls with paintings, shelves with knicknacks and "ornaments." Even animals seem to be receptive to the lure of ornamentation as suggested by the ornamental feathers of the males of certain species of birds, which seem to exert a powerful attraction on the females. But what is the purpose of ornamentation in cases in which the decorated animal lives in permanent darkness or has no eyes, as is the case with many shells?

In nature, what is popularly called ornamentation is, of course, not decorative at all but functional, its purpose being either camouflage, mimicry or warning. The beautiful soft shades and subtle patterns of many mammals, ground-nesting birds, flatfishes and insects make them blend to an uncanny degree with their immediate surroundings; as soon as these animals stop moving, they virtually disappear. And in cases in which the ornamentation consists of brilliant colors and flashy patterns, it often serves as a warning to predators and other enemies: watch out, leave me alone because I taste bad, I am poisonous, I carry a mighty sting! In still other cases it makes a harmless and defenseless insect look like a dangerous or unpalatable one (mimicry). But what about the beautiful ornamental patterns of many butterflies, or those of the shells shown on the next three pages?

Of the purpose of ornamental designs like these, science admits, we know nothing. Nor do we know, for example, why a certain group of scales on a butterfly's wing is red while the adjacent one is blue, or why the linear design of one species of shell is zigzag while that of another one is wavy and that of a third assumes the form of straight bands. Again, we can only say that nature is as creative in regard to ornamental design as she is in regard to structure, texture and form. All else is conjecture.

This lack of understanding, however, does not have to deter us from enjoying these beautiful designs—appreciation is not dependent on knowledge; it is an emotional response.

Opposite: Design detail of a Hebrew cone shell (*Conus ebraeus* Linné).

Above: Bednall's volute (*Volutoconus bednalli* Brazier). *Opposite:* Chocolate flamed Venus (*Lioconcha castrensis* Linné). The purpose of these stunning designs is unknown.

Above: A sphinx moth sleeping the day away on a tree trunk. *Opposite:* A bullhead *(Cottus gobio)*—a fish. In both cases, the purpose of color is obviously protective, color forming a pattern which makes its possessor all but invisible provided, of course, the animal rests on an appropriate surface. What captures my imagination is the degree to which nature, evolution,

natural selection, God—call it what you will—succeeds in camouflaging animals to help them fool their enemies by means of cryptic color or form. Notice, for example, how the rounded head and fins of the bull head resemble the algae-covered pebbles found in most tide pools, or how the elongated wings of the moth mirror the lighter, elongated plates of bark.

Ornament or camouflage? A difficult question that probably must be answered with "both." For there is no doubt that the stripes of the zebra *(above)* form a "disruptive pattern" which, from a distance, makes the animal blend with its background, more difficult for a predator to spot. And the same probably applies to the chambered nautilus *(opposite)*. But what I find particularly interesting is the fact that, in both cases, arrangement and effect of the stripes is identical although one of the creatures is a land-based mammal, the other a mollusk living in the sea.

Man's craving for beauty is as old as humanity itself. The oldest known burials contain evidence that red ochre was used as body paint. Ice Age tools of bone and antler show traces of ornamentation. No wonder, then, that the urge to beautify also extends to the human body, manifesting itself in four specific forms: painting, tattooing, scarification and adornment with such extraneous objects as feathers, jewelry, ranging from nose rings and lip plugs to solitaires, false hair, false eyelashes, false fingernails, false breasts. Today, such cosmetics as lipstick, face powder, rouge, eyeliner, eye shadow, mascara and nail polish are used all over the world. Sailors and longshoremen still practice the art of tattooing, and not so long ago German students deliberately scarified their faces in ceremonial saber duels.

That the roots of these forms of body art reach back to the very beginnings of humanity is evidenced by innumerable statues that have come to us through the ages. On the following pages are photographs of sculptures of women which, in my opinion, are objects of nature in the same sense as nests of birds or hornets, spiderwebs and other animal-originated "artifacts" because they are the instinctive expression of often unsophisticated people who fashioned these statues for ritualistic purposes in accordance with timeless traditions. Simultaneously, despite a certain degree of stylization and abstraction, these figurines are documents insofar as they represent the feminine ideal of their time as seen through the eye of the male—humanity contemplating itself, woman as object of worship and art.

The inch-high ivory carving from the Aurignacian Period shown on the opposite page is between 15,000 and 20,000 years old. Mouthless and silent, with eyes deeply sunk below the brow, it has a timeless expression that casts a fascinating spell. The portrait of a girl, a woman, a seeress, it seems to personify all the sorrow of the world, arising from the wisdom of the transient nature of life. And yet the severity of this little sculpture is relieved by a worldly touch. Already, in the oldest known likenesses of human beings, there is evidence of man's irrepressible craving for beauty: here, the hair arrangement or headdress is patterned in a geometric design, the very first manifestation of conceptual abstract art.

Above: Fetish of the Babembe, Republic of the Congo, Africa (Carlebach 21721). *Opposite:* Head of a statue of a fertility goddess of the Bena Lulua, Zaïre, Africa (Brooklyn Museum, New York; 50–124). Examples of body ornamentation through cicatrization—a kind of three-dimensional tattoo produced by artificial scarification arranged in regular patterns or intricate designs. Some authorities believe that the original purpose of body scarification was deliberately to make the girls and young women of certain African tribes repulsive to Arab slave raiders, who would leave them in peace.

Opposite: Wooden carving from Tchambuli in New Guinea (American Museum of Natural History, New York; 80/7430). *Right:* Wooden figurine from the Bakuba tribe, Zaïre, Africa (American Museum of Natural History, New York: 90-0/5308). Despite the fact that one comes from the South Pacific and the other from Africa, these nineteenth-century female statuettes are spiritually related in their approach to beauty and art, forerunners of our modern ladies who, with face powder, eye shadow, lipstick and rouge, still practice the ancient art of body painting, although on a more restrained level.

Above: Glazed earthenware figurine from Egypt, 26th to 30th Dynasty, 663–341 B.C. (Brooklyn Museum, New York; 37-332-E). *Opposite:* Bronze statuette of Parwati, India, fifteenth century (Museum of Fine Arts, Boston, Mass.; 21-1832). Although separated from each other by twenty centuries and thousands of miles, these two magnificent statues have many features in common: the large, expressive eyes, straight nose, heavy, rounded breasts, narrow waist and richly ornate headdress and necklace—attributes of beauty that are still valued highly today.

Epilogue

Reviewing in my mind this collection of photographs—objects of nature and their relationship to the works of man—I realize more than ever the total interdependence of all things natural and artificial, living and inanimate: how man's world, from technology to art, is based on the materials, designs and laws of nature, and how the course of nature in turn is influenced by the attitude and the actions of man. Sometimes these relationships are subtle and difficult to trace, especially in regard to nature's influence on some of the artifacts of man. On other occasions they are glaring, particularly so far as man's despoliation of nature is concerned: deforesting the land, man creates deserts; polluting the water, poisoning the air and exterminating entire species of animals and plants, he destroys the balance of nature with catastrophic results. But precisely the fact that man is able to subjugate and "control" nature leads many people to believe that he is a superior being endowed with godlike powers, standing above nature's laws.

This is a potentially fatal fallacy. Man is and always will be an integral part of nature, in equal partnership with animals and plants. Protecting the animals and plants, he safeguards his own future; misusing and destroying them, he assures his doom. Today, the truth of this is almost universally accepted, yet few feel the need to act accordingly. Selfishness and greed are rampant. People do not care and often do not even know what they destroy. Money for destruction—euphemistically called development or national defense—is available in almost limitless amounts; for conservation, it is doled out grudgingly.

A large number of books on ecological subjects has been written by informed, concerned people; perhaps too many—the public is nearing the saturation point. A new approach seemed indicated—hence this book. It documents the interdependence of man and nature seen in a different light, with emphasis on the relationship between nature, technique and art. The approach is low-key and positive—instead of predicting impending disaster, I chose a more constructive tone, hoping to open the reader's eyes to the beauty of ordinary things—familiar objects of nature which nevertheless can provide an endless source of joy and inspiration to anyone who cares. This seems to me the key word: CARE. Things for which people care become precious; they will be appreciated, guarded, preserved. If I can convince even a handful of what Loren Eiseley calls the "World-Eaters" of the need for conservation by convincing them that not only our civilization, but our very existence—our survival—depends on taking care of our world, then I feel I did not create this book in vain.